T0381512

Getting Started
in
Track and Field Athletics

Gary Barber

Trafford rev. 10/08/2021

www.trafford.com
North America & international
toll-free: 844-688-6899 (USA & Canada)
fax: 812 355 4082

Getting Started in Track and Field Athletics
Laying the groundwork

Getting Started in Track and Field Athletics
Sprinting

Sprinting — continued

Relay Racing

Getting Started in Track and Field Athletics
Distance Running

Getting Started in Track and Field Athletics

Getting Started in Track and Field Athletics
The Jumps

Getting Started in Track and Field Athletics
The Jumps—continued

The Throwing Events

The Hurdling events

Multi event competitions and Race Walking

Getting Started in Track and Field Athletics

On Your marks!

Walking across the freshly cut grass, smells of Spring hanging in the air, a track and field coach turns his thoughts to the upcoming season. Soon, the white lines will be painted onto the sports field and a running track will magically appear. It is not hard to imagine the sprinters tearing down the straight like miniature lightning bolts – each desperately hoping for athletic success. The coach thinks about his sprint training programs and wonders how effective they will be for the young children he is about to teach.

He then turns his thoughts to the distance runners. He can already see the carefully measured strides of his runners – those human metronomes – flowing easily through each lap. Some children – lithe of body and fleet of foot – find distance running very easy. Other children would be walking on the one lap warm up. The coach considers how he can make track and field an enjoyable sport for those who are decidedly un-athletic.

Get Set!

As he continues his stroll around the sports field he recalls his own athletic career: measures of success and setback. He remembers those that inspired him to achieve his best and is once again reminded that the relay baton has been placed firmly in his hand.

It is time for him to pass it on.

The school bell rings and his students come tearing across the field. Some are bright eyed, eager and willing. Others, unsure of their abilities. The coach rubs his hand with glee. "Let's get going shall we…." **Go!**

> In the Sun that is young once only, Time let me play and be golden.
>
> Dylan Thomas, Welsh Poet.

Getting Started in Track and Field Athletics

How children can use this book.

I hope that the stories in this book will inspire you and that you will enjoy the games that have been created to make track and field athletics really fun. I have included sections throughout the book titled "*Questions that children ask.*" This is for you! I hope the answers will help you to learn more about this sport and will encourage you to give your absolute best effort.

How teachers and coaches can use this book.

Throughout the book you will find small sections titled "*The Teachers Corner*" and "*Coaching Tips.*" These sections are devoted to the linking of track and field ideas with pedagogy and with scientific and educational research. Suggestions for the practical implementation of these ideas into the gymnasium and on the track are included. This book has been written so that you can challenge your capable athletes with knowledge and activities that will take their fitness and skill level forward. However, equally – if not more - important, this book is for the children who find track to be a difficult sport. Activities have been created that can make track fun for athletes of all abilities.

How Parents can use this book.

Parents of elementary-aged school children have been described by psychologists as the "initiators of the sporting experience." This is an attempt to describe the various roles that parents fulfill in the formative years of the child's sporting development. The parent may inspire or comfort their child's experiences. They seek out sports resources (clubs, facilities, etc) sign-up a child and provide equipment. They might be a vociferous mentor, or a quiet supporter. Whatever their motivation, style of interaction, or intentions, it is certain that parents will have a profound impact on the young athlete.

This book includes sections that will address the issues and answer questions that parents consider when deciding to "sign-up" their child for track and field athletics.

Getting Started in Track and Field Athletics
Laying the ground work

Although Bruce Springsteen would beg otherwise, *we were not born to run!* It takes your average child several years to learn the basic elements of movement and balance while progressing slowly from a crawl to a walk, and then a run. As soon as the child starts to run they adapt to balance and coordination problems by moving their limbs in ways that increases their movement stability. Many of these movement patterns are counter- productive to effective track and field athletics. One of the first challenges for the coach is to help athletes recognise how their body moves when running and identify ways to improve their movement efficiency. Teaching young athletes the correct techniques is an important part of track and field program. To address these issues, each section of the book is organised in the following way:

- The various techniques of each event and the common mistakes that are made are reviewed
- Games and activities that can bring fun into your program are covered
- The history of each event is covered
- Questions that children and parents ask are answered

Getting Started in Track and Field Athletics
The stages of a child's athletic development

Some of the most frequently asked questions / issues that perplex parents is when to start their child in a particular activity; *"Is she too young?" "Is he too advanced for this group?"* etc. Chronology—i.e. how old the child is—has never been a good indicator of a child's readiness for a particular activity. Understanding the stages of development that all children will go through may help guide parents as they face these issues.

Some exercise scientists have suggested that there are critical or sensitive periods of a child's athletic development . Providing activities that are rich in challenges to the balance and sensory systems are appropriate for very young children. Activities that enhance coordination and movement mechanics are beneficial for the age-group 5—12 years. It has been suggested that it is difficult to compensate (i.e. brings skills to a good standard) from a lack of development during these critical periods.

Implication: The coach / teacher should ensure that all the sports activities in this period are rich with opportunities to develop coordination skills, activities that promote balance (gymnastics, using playground apparatus), rhythm (dance), spatial awareness (games of tag, etc), and fitness (basic conditioning).

The Teachers Corner
Why do kids participate in sport?

The following results are taken from two surveys with almost 6,000 children - girls and boys in equal numbers - ages 7 –12. The reason I participate in sport is to.....

1. Have Fun
2. Improve my skills
3. To do something that I'm good at.
4. Have the excitement of competition
5. To get exercise
6. To play with my team
7. To enjoy the challenge of competition

Getting Started in Track and Field Athletics
At what age should my athletes start training?

Grade 2 — This should purely be an introduction to track and field. Students can be taught the principles of starting, they will enjoy racing each other over short distances. The rules of sprinting can be easily introduced. Three—four sessions of 30 minutes per week centered around fun games, racing, and relays. The emphasis is on participation and not outcomes.

Grade 3 — At this grade, the students can be introduced to elements of technique: sprint starting, using blocks, incorporating relaxation into their running. The rules, tactics of racing can be developed. 3 / 4 sessions of 30 minutes per week is plenty of practise for this age. Activities that help to develop coordination should be a feature of these practise sessions. Although some children will find sprint drills to be difficult, they will undoubtedly help improve coordination.

Grade 4 — The students of this age –group are increasingly able to benefit from the basic principles of fitness development. 3/ 4 sessions of 40 minutes per week centered on some fitness work, fun games, and activities will be beneficial for these students.

Grade 5 — the amount of practise that this age group is comparable to grade 4 but the students should be able to produce a higher quality of performance.

Grade 6 — These students are starting to enter puberty and any training program should accommodate the changing growth patterns of the child. With any of these recommendations for training programs, it should be acknowledged that they are generic (i.e. for your average class), a more effective program would be one that is tailored to the individual. Some children have precocious growth patterns and may be ready for a more intense and involved program. Other students may require careful nurturing before they are ready for hard training.

Getting Started in Track and Field Athletics
Questions that parents ask...
Will my child get injured?

There are primarily two sources of athletic injury: those that occur from accidents and those that occur from over use. It is primarily the responsibility of the coach / teacher to ensure that the training environment is a safe one— and thereby limit the chances for accidents. Children of elementary age should not be getting overuse injuries. If they are, the stress load of the child should be examined and the parent needs to consider whether it is appropriate that the child be practising so much. Common overuse injuries include tendonitis, excessive muscular soreness and stress on the growth plates. Osgood—Schlatters disease of the knee can be prompted by too much physical stress on the joint. A degree of muscular soreness is common as children (and adults) adapt to exercise. It is when it becomes excessive and inhibits natural movement that it becomes problematic. It is advisable to consult with a sports physician if your child is experiencing any of these issues.

Will my child peak too soon?

The reality is that athletes will likely reach their peak levels of performance in their 20's not in their pre-teens! Of course, many active young children will not persist in this sport through their teen years and into their 20's— this occurs for a myriad of complex social reasons. Sadly, many talented athletes never fully realise their potential. *What if a child is experiencing some measure of success?* Of course they are not at their peak, some of this success may be due to diligent practise or the simple fact that they have grown earlier than their opponents. The coach / parent should thus keep childhood success in its perspective: it is nice to do well but undue pressure and unrealistic expectations can only serve to undermine the athlete's healthy development.

Emphasize the joys of participation, and by make the practises fun you will be doing a great service to the athlete.

Getting Started in Track and Field Athletics

From development to high performance - at what age should my child specialize in track and field (sport)?

The myths and realities of sport often mix and blur the answer to this question. Ask a parent who sees dollar signs in the eyes of their child and you will get a different answer to the one I am about to offer. Likewise with the coach that wants to build "a winning program" with his 8 year olds! With a quick scan of community sports programs you can find plenty of evidence of coaches or parents who are training / pushing their youngsters to specialize at an very early age in a particular sport. Interestingly, if you read the profiles of many of the greatest athletes in the world, most came to their sport in their teenage years and in childhood, they were very active pursuing many different types of activity. The risks of early specialization clearly outweigh advantages - injury, burnout, a narrow range of general skills is not the language of success in later years.

So, to answer the question, when is it appropriate to apply specialized training programs? The answer will depend on the sport, but for track and field the introduction can start at the age of 7 years with fun games and activities, knowledge and basic skill building until 12. Further development continues through teenage years with the introduction of special training and then high level performance as an adult (typically mid 20's).

Questions Children Ask...

How do I run in the Olympics?

The Olympic Games is a sports festival that is held once every four years. For the track competition, each country may enter 3 athletes as long as they have achieved a qualifying standard—that is they have run a race in a certain time. So, an athlete must be in the top three in their country and perform to a high standard. For a young person dreaming of competing in the Olympics I would encourage you to join a club and concentrate on having fun in what you do. As you grow older and into your teenage years you can then start to practice hard. Never let go of that dream—many of the world's greatest athletes started with a dream just like yours!

Getting Started in Track and Field Athletics
Identifying your talented athletes—a mirage on the track?

When it comes to the identification of sporting talent all is not what it seems. Some young children enjoy success because they are simply more biologically advanced than their opponents—i.e. they have started to grow earlier than another athlete. Biological development and the athlete's age are significant influences on performance in young children. It does not always follow that your successful athlete is the most naturally talented. Some children in the same school year can be up to 12 months older than other children— obviously, this can place some children at significant advantages over others.

Success at a young age—while enjoyable for the athlete (and the proud parents) - in the grand scheme of development it is not particularly meaningful. Puberty is often the great equaliser; as bodies can drastically change shape the diminutive child at the child at the back may suddenly power forward and express their hidden talents for sport. In the same way, the star athlete no longer enjoys the biological advantages of precocious development and now actually has to work hard for success. Success in sport is certainly to be enjoyed but it is not uncommon to find some children run much slower times during puberty than when they were younger.

Getting Started in Track and Field Athletics
A recipe for success

I term the key ingredients of a good track program the ..'tions: *Inspiration, dedication, motivation, determination, and perspiration*. The emphasis on each ingredient shifts according to the skills and age of the children that you are coaching. For the young athletes your track program should be structured play, thus the key ingredients needed here are inspiration and motivation. Good stories, fun games that enhance fitness, and motivational devices – ribbons, goals, challenges, can create an atmosphere of success for each child.

The perspiration ingredient – the hard training that is needed to reach a standard, is a component that is more suited for when the athlete has grown and is physically capable able to adapt to your program. For teenagers this component is important so long as it is incrementally applied. Good coaches also help their athletes to reach their potential by shaping the character and values of the athlete. Good role modeling and inspirational stories can have a profound influence on a developing athlete.

Like any good recipe, too much or too little of any ingredient can spoil the product: Food for thought!

Getting Started in Track and Field Athletics

The stages of learning a new track and field skill

Stage 1 - The skill is introduced. The athlete will bring a certain attitude to learning this new skill—the motivated will embrace the challenge, the un-athletic may be hesitant. Using demonstrations may help the conceptual understanding of the skill. Coaches should avoid excessive repetitions as this will create fatiguing (both mentally and physically) and interfere with learning.

Stage 2 - The action is performed. Some children will execute the skill with a close approximation of the desired result, others will be way off. Techniques to help keep the un-athletic motivated on-task are covered in this book.

Stage 3 -The skill is corrected, refined, and practised. Many sources of informational feedback can be used. Recognising our new understanding of different learning styles (Gardner's Multiple Intelligence theory) information should be presented in ways that appeals to visual and auditory, and kinaesthetic styles of learning.

Stage 4- The skill is practised in a closed environment, i.e. outside of competition. This allows for further refinement of the skill.

Stage 5 - The skill is now applied in a competitive environment.
according to Frank Dick (1976)

Example : Learning a sprint start

Stage 1 - Use words and visual techniques to introduce the concept and point out the relevant technical issues.
Stage 2—Practise sprinting starts. 6 x 30 m concentrate on technique. Get out of the blocks fast, etc. The coach advises on errors and recognises correct movement.
Stage 3 - Refinement of technique. The coach may use video cameras as a feedback tool. Peer and self assessment helps all kids to become more aware of their skills.
Stage 4– 5 Practise with competitions amongst friends and then rivals

Getting Started in Track and Field Athletics

When children join a track and field program they do not want to stand still. They want to run and they want to release lots of energy.; above all, they want to have fun. Here are some pointers to help plan for a class / workout:

Get them active immediately. As soon as the children arrive in the class, have a game of tag, a few races, anything that focuses their abundant energy on a task. If you sit the children on the benches / floor while waiting for any stragglers to emerge from the changing rooms, etc, you are not only wasting valuable time, but also inviting mischief from those kids eager to be active.

Kids want to have feedback on their performances – letting children know how they have performed is very important to them. Never assume that the child who has finished dead last in a run is any less interested on their performance than the kid that finished first. Various techniques can be used to assess performance: video tape analysis highlighting skill attainment is very popular with children. Peer assessment, self assessment, criteria based assessment, all help to guide children towards better performances.

Keep your instruction time succinct – Too much technical talk and you will lose your audience. Children are certainly eager to learn, they want tips on how to improve their performance, but they want to spend most of their time actually doing the event – not listening on how to do it! Coaching effectiveness is maximised by understanding the attention spans of your class.

> With this age group, it is important not stress outcomes but effort and the mastery of various skills.

Getting Started in Track and Field Athletics

Answering the following questions may help you structure your practices and coaching advice in such ways that the motivate and inspire your un-athletic children.

Massed versus distributed practice?

Do you schedule your practices into learning bundles, or space them out to allow time for the children to learn skills and 'digest" information / skills?

It is important to remember that practice alone is not a guarantee of learning. Do your students know when they are performing a newly learned skill correctly? Have you communicated to your students why this is an important skill? How does it fit into the "big picture?" Is it fun practising this skill?

Massing your practise sessions is where you practise the skill repeatedly over several days. One benefit of this approach is that it increases the chances of the skill being quickly learned. The risk however is that without correction a bad habit may be reinforced. Distributing the practises - i.e. spacing the practise of this skill allows for variety and a new energy to be applied to skill learning. The risk here, however, is that if you space your practises too far apart, the learning may quickly decay without further reinforcement.

How do you un-learn bad technique and replace it with something that will produce better results? How long will this take?

Verbal descriptions, role modeling correct movement (either by the coach or by another athlete) may be useful but I have found to be very effective is to use videotape analysis. Filming the children sprint and then analysing performance is a useful teaching tool. Once the athlete has identified spurious movement patterns, the challenge for the coach and athlete is to devise teaching and learning strategies to re-educate the athlete. Correct technique is discussed in each of the events covered throughout this book.

Getting Started in Track and Field Athletics

Creating a safe track environment

Train the children in track and field etiquette, this will include:

- Treating the track like a road: don't run across it without looking to see if anything (or anyone is coming).

- Warm-up in the outer lanes of the track—not lane 1 where other athletes may be racing or training.

- Always walk with track and field equipment (shot puts, high jump bars, etc).

- Have a maximum of 15 runners on a start line. You may have more if you hold a split-start— i.e. you use the stagger of the outer lanes with a break for the inside after 100m. This feature is sometimes used in distance races from 800m up.

- Examine the track (especially if it is a school sports field) looking for potholes.

- If you are using a starting gun, **never allow a student to even touch the gun.** Some starting pistols discharge an immense pressure wave. Even though the gun is firing a blank charge, there have been a number of deaths and brain injuries to people who have fired the gun against their head believing no harm could happen to them. Cap guns or whistles are a safer way to start the race.

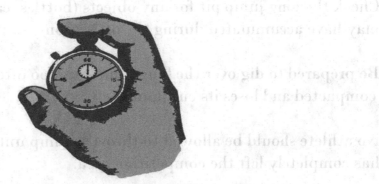

Getting Started in Track and Field Athletics
Creating a safe field event environment

Risk assessment of the facility and the equipment is always the starting-point for determining a safe environment. The rules of common sense should preclude the majority of incidents; e.g. "don't throw the shot put toward your friend!" However, when fatalities have occurred a number of consistent themes emerge from inquiries. The first is what has been dubbed "the imaginary fable." This is a mindset that believes that bad things only occur to other people. The contributors to the accident failed to identify the potential risks and consequences of their actions. A lack of structure or understanding of what constitutes safe practice also contributed to these accidents. Educate your athletes to understand that the infield of the track should be respected as a place where potential danger exists if field events (especially the throws) are taking place. It is incumbent on teachers / coaches to train their parent volunteers in these safety practices. Some specifics to address:

- Carry heavy objects (like shot puts) with two hands.

- Rope a 45 degree vector to keep athletes well away from the throwing zone in shot put.

- Officiously orchestrate the transition from one athlete leaving the throwing circle / or long jump pit

- Many field event officials use a single blast on a small trumpet to indicate when a throw is about to take place, followed by two blasts to indicate when it is safe.

- Check the long jump pit for any objects (bottles, cans, cat-poo, etc) that may have accumulated during the off-season

- Be prepared to dig over the long jump pit. Too often the sand gets compacted and loses its cushioning effect.

- No athlete should be allowed to throw or jump until a previous athlete has completely left the competition area.

Getting Started in Track and Field Athletics

Winning and losing : It's all about perspective!

It seems that too often our society takes extreme views on issues and sport, it seems, is no different. When it comes to sporting competition we have seen pop culture suggest *"2nd place is first loser!" "Winning isn't the only thing, it's everything."* The message for the tens of thousands of children is clear: those of you who will never win a race, a long jump competition, a shot put event, might as well not bother! This is an appalling concept and the sports advertising agencies who have promoted this message have done a great disservice to the youth of the nation.

The pendulum often swings in extremes before it settles in the middle.

In the book *"Alice in Wonderland"* Alice observes an event called *"The Caucaus Race."* People run about Wonderland in a completely disorganized manner and in any direction. They are then all declared to be winners of the race. Some school districts have banned all forms of competition (including such staples as the egg and spoon race, or the sack race) at elementary school sports. And yet children will still create ways to find out who won! Children expect authenticity in sports competitions. They all know that the object of the event is to win but (amazing to many adults as it may seem) that is not their primary purpose in participation.

This book recommends the following— the middle ground:

- It is okay to want to win the track and field event but a greater emphasis on effort and mastering skills should be made.

- If the coach / parent / teacher can create a fun and positive atmosphere outcomes and rewards can become less important.

Sprinting

"Now bid me run and I shall strive for things impossible."
Shakespeare

Getting Started in Track and Field Athletics
The History of Sprinting

Mankind has run – sprinted – for tens of thousands of years. The earliest records of running can be found in the paintings on the cave walls at Lascaux, France. They clearly show people chasing animals or being chased ! Historical records that pre-date the ancient Greeks are scarce, but it is probably safe to assume that throughout time the desire to compete had a powerful influence on early mankind. Quite simply, if you were not fast enough to beat your rival to an animal and then strong enough to kill it, your family went hungry.

Greece is considered by Sports Historians to be the home of organised athletic competition. From the years 796 bc until 393 AD, organised games – especially the Olympic Games – gave warriors the opportunity to test their skills in sport. Running, jumping, wrestling, throwing the javelin were integral parts of the games.

Track Trivia
Aethelius, the King of Elis – a small state near Olympia, Greece – was such an ardent supporter of sport that he allowed his name to be used to describe the people who took part in such sports – thus they became known as Athletes.

Getting Started in Track and Field Athletics

In order to honour the gods that oversaw the games, the King of Elis demanded that sacrificial offerings (mainly fruits and vegetables) were made to Zeus. Young athletes then raced each other for flaming torches that were then carried to the altar to light a fire in completion of the sacrifice. Some historians suggest that this was the first Olympic sprint race. The winner of the race earned the right to wear the much coveted laurel or olive wreath around their head and were given sticks of celery as their prize. In later games, money was awarded as the prize and this started to bring cheating into the games. Can you imagine that in today's Olympics – *" and the winner of the 100m gets a bunch of celery sticks!"*

The shape of today's Olympic Games still reflect the ancient games practices. The sprint race was considered a premium event and would cover a distance of almost 200m – or *1 stade* which is Greek for short foot race. Two *stades* was the equivalent of a 400m race and this was known as a Diaulos.

Getting Started in Track and Field Athletics

Equipment not necessary!

When the athlete Orsippos tripped over his shorts (that had fallen down) during the sprint race, it started a trend at the ancient Olympic Games that lasted for centuries: nude running. As the Greeks admired the beauty of athletic performance—thus our modern phrase "poetry in motion" - just as much as the outcome of the race, nude running was completely normal. History records that Orsippos ripped off his shorts, jumped up, and went onto win the sprint race! While clothing might have been optional, there were some rules that you just should not break: athletes were not allowed to cheat, bribe officials, or cast magical spells on their rivals!

There is no greater glory for a man in all his life than
what he achieves with his own feet and hands.

Homer — The Odyssey

Getting Started in Track and Field Athletics

The need for speed!

At major track and field events, sprinting is considered to be one of the **blue ribbon events**- something with immense prestige attached to it. The title: The World's Fastest Man / Woman is often given to the champions at such events. Unlike sports that determine the winner by the judge's opinion, sprinting celebrates pure athleticism: the title goes to the first across the line (unless they cheat by using drugs – but don't get me started on that one!).

Sprint events in the Summer track and field season include 100m, 200, and 400m. In the indoor season distances vary but the 60m sprint is the most common distance. The hurdles -100m for women and 110m for men, plus 400m hurdles are also considered sprint events but these will not be covered here. This section of the book suggests sprint training methods for young children for 100m and 200m. Although 400m running is also considered a sprint race, there is currently some debate over the appropriateness of 400m running for young children. 400m has a significant anaerobic energy demand (the rich energy source that the body produces in the absence of oxygen). It is clear that young children have very poorly developed anaerobic energy systems and find this event very demanding. 400m racing also requires a well defined sense of pace judgement to prevent early fatiguing. Sprinting flat out from the very beginning has proven to be counter productive for even the most brilliant of high level athletes. And yet, that seems to be the preferred (and only) tactic of the young and inexperienced athlete. Quickly, they fatigue and struggle to complete the race. Thus training techniques for the 400m is not within the scope of this book.

Why is the 100m sprint sometimes called a Blue Ribbon event?

In 1651 the British army decided that the morale and fitness of the soldiers could be tested in sporting competitions. Soldiers who won their events were given a blue ribbon to wear as a symbol of their success. Today, a blue ribbon event is a term given to athletic competitions that some people consider to have great importance. The Olympic Games 100m is a blue ribbon event as the winner is not only the champion but also earns the title of the world's fastest human (on that day).

Getting Started in Track and Field Athletics

If you raced these animals over 100m...

A Cheetah would run the 100m in 3.20 seconds reaching a peak speed of 60 miles per hour.

A Reindeer would run the 100m in 6.99 seconds averaging 32 miles per hour.

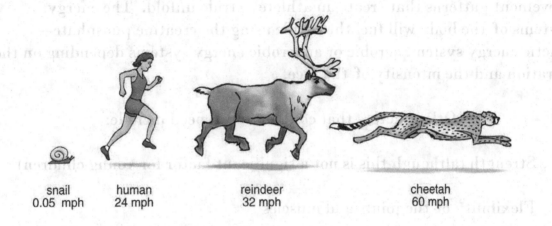

snail	human	reindeer	cheetah
0.05 mph	24 mph	32 mph	60 mph

Asafa Powell —the fastest man in the world—would run 100m in 9.77 seconds with a peak speed 26.95 miles per hour.

Florence Griffith Joyner— the fastest woman in the world — would run 100m in 10.49 seconds with a peak speed of 24.58 miles per hour.

An athletic snail would "run" the 100m in 2 hours averaging 0.05 miles per hours!

How fast can you run the 100m?

Getting Started in Track and Field Athletics

What makes a runner move fast?

Speed is the product of the rapid movement of muscles and joints in a particular direction. To create speed, a series of co-ordinated actions within the athlete's body need to take place. When we start to sprint our brain sends signal through the nervous system and instructs the muscles to start moving—hopefully fast! Some muscles will contract at great speed and others will be instructed to relax as the sequence of sophisticated movement patterns that create an athlete's stride unfold. The energy systems of the body will fuel this stride using the creatine phosphate—alactic energy system, aerobic or anaerobic energy systems depending on the duration and the intensity of the race.

Other factors that contribute to speed include:

- Strength (although this is not a significant factor for young children)

- Flexibility of the joints and muscles

- Reaction time - how quickly can the athlete respond to the sound of the gun

Body morphology (shape) plays a role in the athlete's ability to reach a good standard of speed.

Getting Started in Track and Field Athletics

Nature – Nurture and the World's fastest runners

A debate about sprinters (and our general development) that has lasted centuries is whether great athletes are made (i.e. trained) or created (i.e. born with the ability to be the fastest)? The science of muscle biopsy has given us a few hints that can help you to clarify your views on this debate. Biopsies have also provided a greater understanding as to how muscles work and the possibilities or limits of athletic performance. A muscle biopsy is where a long—but thin needle is inserted into the muscle (often the thigh) and a sample of the athlete's tissue is then removed and studied with a high powered microscope. Sprinters predominately have white muscle fibres. These fibres "twitch" or move very rapidly and help the athlete to reach top speed. However these fibres can only maintain this speed for a short time before they start to reach exhaustion. Other muscle fibres are red, these "twitch" at a slower speed than the whites but can keep working much longer than a white fibre. The red fibres are commonly found in distance runners.

The number of red or white muscle fibres cannot be changed but they can be trained. Specific training techniques can improve the efficiency at which these fibres work. Fortunately sports performances are not decided in the science lab—a distance runner with very well trained red and white fibres (everybody has a mix of both fibres) may be able to out sprint an athlete with more white fibres that are untrained. Will one athlete with many more white fibres (nature—i.e. they are born with the disposition to sprint) defeat an athlete with a limited number of white fibres but has practiced hard (nurture—i.e. they have improved their abilities to sprint) ? As there are many complex factors that shape the athlete's performance—training, motivation, state of health, climate, diet, to name but a few— the answer to the nature versus nurture is rife with contradictions. Given the specific training demands of some events, I think it is safe to assume that a world class marathon runner will not out –run a world class sprinter and vice versa. At the school level the issue blurs as fitness and state of biological development can play a leading role in performance.

Getting Started in Track and Field Athletics

The phases of a sprint race

Every single sprinting race has the following components:

- The Start of the race (the reaction phase)
- Acceleration phase
- Maximum speed phase
- Deceleration phase
- Finish of the race

Athletes who train for this event will need to practise each phase both separately and collectively to produce a good standard of performance. Deficit in one area is unlikely to be remedied by over compensation in another e.g. a poor start is difficult to recover from in the 100m.

The start of the race (the reaction phase)

There is more to starting a sprint race than a simple: On your marks, Get set, Go! At the highest levels of this sport, athletes will use starting blocks to assist their start. They will carefully place them on the track and await the starter's command to come to the start line. The athletes can take a reasonable amount of time to settle into their start positions. If the athlete takes too long to settle they can be awarded a false start (essentially for delaying the start of the race)

What is the advantage of sprint starting?

Sprint starting allows the runner to quickly find a bio-mechanically efficient running position (which translates into english as.. the runner can start to run fast quicker using this technique than an athlete using a standing start.) Why? Because the sprint start position shifts the athlete's centre of gravity forward. This will cause the runner to fall flat on their face unless they rapidly move their legs forward to counter act gravity.

Getting Started in Track and Field Athletics

The evolution of starting techniques

The athletes in the ancient Olympic games used several techniques to start in the Stades race (short foot race over 192m). The first technique saw runners standing with their feet together. In today's races, it is hard to imagine an Olympic athlete standing with feet together and hoping to get a really fast start! A few years later a Sill (or Balipides) was created to act like starting blocks. The Sill was essentially a slab of marble in the ground with hollow lines carved into it. The athlete would stand and place one foot into the line and push against it when the race started. The races at the ancient Olympic Games were started by the blast of a Herald's trumpet and the shout "*Apite!*" Runners did not dare to false start for fear of receiving a beating from the Alyte— a policeman!

Note the concrete sill in this picture and the trumpet in the background.

Before starting blocks were created, an essential part of a sprinters equipment was a small garden trowel. There is an interesting scene in the film "Chariots of Fire" where the runners are preparing for the Olympic sprint final. Each runner is carefully digging two small holes with a garden trowel into the cinder track. The runners then place their feet into the holes and will push against them when the race starts.

Getting Started in Track and Field Athletics

In this picture, the great Jesse Owens (Olympic Champion for 100m, 200m and long jump at the Berlin Games, 1936) is in his "get set" position. Note that he is not using starting blocks but has dug two small holes into the cinder track.

In the early 1900's starting sticks became the fashion in sprinting races. Athletes would bring two small wooden sticks that they could lean on in their "get set position!" Runners leaning too far forward often found the sticks could not hold their weight and would make them off balance at the start. Starting sticks did not stay around for long!

Getting Started in Track and Field Athletics

What are starting blocks?

Starting blocks were invented in 1928 by two American track coaches George Breshnahan and William Tuttle (USA) who were interested in helping athletes get fast starts in their races. Starting blocks (picture below) have been designed to give the athlete a firm platform to push against when the starting gun is fired. At the highest levels of this sport all athletes in sprint races (up to and including 400m) will use starting blocks. The blocks themselves can slide along the bottom metal plate—thus the athlete can adjust them according to their personal preference. The metal plate can sometimes have short metal teeth that bite into the ground (if you are racing on a grass or cinder track). Very long nails may also be used to help anchor the blocks to the ground. On a rubber track pre-set holes are located in the track and the athlete must insert their blocks in these holes — but the athlete can adjust the block if necessary.

There are essentially 3 types of sprint start with starting blocks:
- Bunched or bullet start
- Medium start
- Elongated start

These positions refer to the way the athlete places their body in starting blocks. With the bullet start, the athlete's toes of the rear foot are level with the heel of the front foot. When the athlete takes the get set position their hips are very high and legs "bunched together." The medium starting block technique has the athlete placing their rear knee level with the toes of the front foot. The elongated starting block technique has the rear knee level with the heel of the front foot.

Getting Started in Track and Field Athletics

The runners prepare themselves for the start of the race. They await the starter's commands and focus their thoughts on getting an excellent start

On your marks! The race starter has called these athletes to the start line. They settle into their starting blocks and relax. They concentrate on the starter's command to move into the "get set!" position.

Get Set! The runner on the far left has false started. The other 2 runners are in the correct position and await the firing of the starter's gun. The race starter will start the whole series of steps again, hopefully this athlete will wait for the gun (or else he will be disqualified!)

Go! This time, there are no false starts and the runners start to accelerate. They will reach their top speed within 30m.

Getting Started in Track and Field Athletics

Starting blocks can provide an effective start when the athlete:

- Pushes hard against the block at the firing of the gun. If they do not, there is no point using the blocks—they might as well do a standing start.

- The force that the applies when the gun is fired (i.e. how hard they push) should be applied through the ankle, knee, and hip joints. The athlete should rise out of the blocks at a 45 degree angle.

- The angle of the athlete when in the get set position is important. If they are too high or too low the athlete will fail to receive the benefits of pushing hard against the blocks.

Track Trivia

Every aspect of this short race has been scientifically analysed to find the optimum techniques and training methods for high performance. Russian exercise scientists have even calculated the exact angles of the knee in the starting position (for those of you with a taste for power trivia: 100 degrees for the front starting leg, 129 degrees for the rear starting leg!)

Getting Started in Track and Field Athletics

Questions parents and teachers ask..

At what age should starting blocks be introduced?

The children that I have coached love using starting blocks. They feel as if they are top athletes and really concentrate on using the blocks properly. I have used starting blocks as early as Grade 3— of course with mixed results. However, by the time the students reach Grade 5 have some experience with the blocks and can use them to their advantage.

Do I really need to buy this equipment?

It is not necessary to buy a set of starting blocks (which can cost up to $150). Many of the track stadiums will provide blocks for all athletes to use. It is important to note that if an athlete hasn't learned how to properly use the blocks they are better advised not to use them. At the highest levels of the sport, the athletes have no choice—they must use blocks.

Getting Started in Track and Field Athletics

The role of the race starter

The race starter has an assistant who walks along the start line and ensures that all athletes have their hands and feet completely behind the start line. An athlete may be asked to move a finger or foot off the white start line—if they refuse, they can be awarded a false start. When the assistant is satisfied that everybody is behind the line, a flag is raised and the starter raises the gun. At all times, athletes must be perfectly still on the start line—if they twitch in an attempt to spook an opponent into a false start (and yes this has happened a lot in major events) - the instigator and not the responder is given the false start.

With the command Get Set! the athletes raise their hips high in the air while maintaining four point contact with the track (i.e. both hands and feet). The athletes must be perfectly still. If the starter is satisfied that everybody is still the gun is fired. The delay between get set and the gun being fired is usually no more than a second or two. Before the days of electronic timing, athletes would try to anticipate the firing of the gun and run a fraction before it was fired.

Questions Children Ask...

Is the starter's gun real and does it fire real bullets?

The starter's gun is a very dangerous implement and should only be held by a responsible adult. Such is the force released when a blank cartridge (shell) is fired that it is capable of causing serious injury. This gun is not capable of firing bullets as it does not have a hollow barrel. Sometimes cap guns are used and can be a safe and effective alternative to the gun. At major track events, the starter's gun is connected to an electronic timing device that starts to record the athletes performances when the gun is fired.

Reaction Times

In today's sprint races, the athlete uses starting blocks that are electronically wired to a timing clock. If a runner reacts to the sound of the gun faster than 0.12 seconds, the athlete is deemed to have false started.

Getting Started in Track and Field Athletics

Common mistakes children make in starting

- Falling or stumbling at the start
- Not pushing hard with the rear leg
- Not pushing with the correct leg.
- Standing straight up from a crouched position
- Wrong hands in position for standing start
- Do not drive their arms

How to correct these mistakes

Falling at the start is often caused by the athlete taking too long a first step. If your athlete is repeatedly making this mistake video tape them and have them view their performance.

Skill and practise with using the starting blocks will help overcome the mistake of not pushing hard with a leg. I tell my students that the starting blocks do not provide energy, they only return what you push into them. We use the spring metaphor to describe this point. The children are told that their legs are like springs—if you push a spring together you put lots of energy into it. When you let go of the spring the energy is released. By pushing hard against the blocks the athlete invokes that good old principle of Newtonian physics *"for every action there is an equal and opposite reaction"* - or re-phrased for the athlete using starting blocks –**you only get out what you put in!**

One of the most common mistakes that children make when they are starting a sprint race is that they stand straight up when moving out of the sprint start position. If they do this, the athlete will lose the benefit of this starting position and might as well stand start. Your athletes should be encourage to "stay low coming out of the blocks!"

Swinging the arms in a powerful but relaxed motion helps to generate forward motion. Have your athletes practise loosely swinging their arms. Looking to see your rivals is difficult to avoid for young athletes. Simple command spoken with authority *"look ahead, don't look at your rival"* may help train these runners to avoid this bad but natural habit.

The acceleration phase of sprinting

When the gun is fired, forward movement is initiated by the powerful extension of the back leg. The torso (the chest) should at a 45 degree angle to the ground but will quickly rise with each subsequent step. The first step that is taken should be short as this will allow power to be applied through the limb and enable the athlete to accelerate quickly. This is like accelerating on a bicycle—low gears enable you to pick up speed, then you switch to higher gears for top speed. If an athlete's stride length is too long in the first few strides, they cannot accelerate as fast as with a shorter stride.

The athlete's acceleration is assisted by vigorous swinging of the arms. The emphasis should be on the back swing. Encourage your athletes to keep their heads still and their shoulders relaxed. As speed is generated, there will be the tendency for the young sprinter to strain i.e. they believe that the harder they try the faster they will go. Again, relaxation should be encouraged.

Coaching Tips

Australian sports scientists have determined that the first 6—8 strides of the sprint represent the acceleration phase. After the 8th stride, the athlete should have reached maximum speed. When practising acceleration, there is no need for the athlete to go too much further than 10 strides of flat out running.

Getting Started in Track and Field Athletics

What are the common mistakes that children make when accelerating?

Over-striding — Young children often take excessively long strides as they try to accelerate to top speed. Using camcorders can help the athlete see how they are over-striding and the need to correct this problem.

Under-striding — taking short pitter-patter steps—lots of speed but covering very little ground. The athletes should be introduced to the concept of the optimum stride length and consider if their current form matches that ideal. Video recording of an athlete's technique is a useful device to help them recognize the flaws in the sprinting skill.

Excessive effort — straining hard to reach top speed but the muscular tension that results from this type of effort is actually counter productive to fast sprinting. In a later section of this book, there is a piece that reviews the importance of relaxation to reach top sprinting speed. Young children often make the mistake of trying harder and harder to reach their best speed and in doing so, become very tense and consequently run much slower.

Coaching Tips

Technique is such an important part of sprinting. During the acceleration phase young athletes will often strain to reach top speed and abandon the correct skills that they have been taught. Wild swinging of the arms, rotational body movements can occur. The teacher should have the athlete rehearse accelerating but have them concentrate less on top speed, but more on utilizing the correct technique. Eventually, top speed can be achieved with the assistance of efficient running form.

Getting Started in Track and Field Athletics

Abandoning skills — The frustration of a teacher's existence. Having spent much time teaching and practicing the skills, they are not used in competitions. Sometimes a firm reminder is needed to ensure that the children will apply the skills that they have been taught.

Lack of confidence — Applying new skills in successful ways requires a degree of self confidence. It is common for young children to resort to the skills that have served them well before (a comfort zone) rather than takes risks in applying their new skills. This will be especially true for the athlete whom does not excel.

Excessive body lean — Leaning too far forward or backward are postures often adopted by young children. A slight forward lean of between 4—6 degrees is recommended.

The maximum and decelerating speed phase of sprinting

For most athletes, maximum speed is reached between 40—60m. Once this is achieved the challenge is to hold this speed for as long as possible. Young athletes may run with the belief that they will run faster and faster until they reach the finishing line. Regrettably, this is not the case—not even for the fastest sprinters in the world. After 60m, all sprinters start to slow down. At both maximum speed and decelerating speed, the challenge for the runner is to maintain their technique as long as possible. Vigorous arm actions, powerful extensions of the rear leg, applying sprinting forces through the ball of the foot (and not the toes), will all help to hold the speed as long as possible. Some people observe that great sprinters start to pull away from other runners toward the finishing line—this is because these athletes are not slowing down as fast as their opponents.

Common mistakes made by young children in this phase of the race include:

• Straining to hold the pace—the increased muscular tension acts like a brake and actually slows the athlete even further.

• Looking over to see how well a rival is doing.

The finish of the sprint race

All phases of a sprint race are important but the finishing phase has probably the greatest potential for success to be won or lost. The last 30m of the sprint race sees all athletes starting to lose their top speed. During this phase the athlete now has concentrate on the coordinated techniques of good sprinting form so as to minimize this deceleration.

Common mistakes in the finish phase

• *Straining to increase speed.* The key to correcting this mistake is to recognize that all athletes are decelerating once they reach this point in the race. The goal for the sprinter is to try to maintain the speed that they have reached for as long as possible. Relaxation and good sprinting technique will help them to this end.

• *Losing technique.* Maintaining your sprinting form at the end of a race requires disciplined concentration. Athletes that practice this skill in training will find it much easier to apply in race situations than athletes that neglect mental skills. The coach can give the athlete instructions to focus on a particular aspect of technique on a practice run. Repeated practice will help hone the mental skills.

• *Clenching muscles.* This is a function of fatigue and the athlete straining to gain an advantage over a rival. Again, practicing relaxation while running at top speed will help the athlete overcome this mistake.

- *Allowing head to wobble or tilt backwards.* Excessive head lean can increase muscular tension in the neck and the shoulders. This in turn will reduce the efficiency of the arm movements and slow the athlete. Train the athlete to keep their head still and looking straight forward.

- *Legs no longer swing in a straight line.* Athletes whom are starting to tire will lose form (i.e.—their running technique starts to deteriorate). The fatiguing—especially in a poorly conditioned athlete is compounded by a lack of concentration. Athletes can limit the effects of fatigue — of which leg swing action is an example — by relying on good technique to see them through to the finishing line.

- *Failure to sprint all the way through the finishing line.* "The race is not over till it's over." This sport cliché particularly rings true for track races. The history of the sport is replete with examples of athletes who failed to run all the way through the finishing line and were beaten by a rival whom would otherwise been defeated.

- *Dip finishing too early.* The dip finish is an essential part of the sprint race but some inexperienced athletes will lean for the line even though they are several metres away from it. Practise and timing are key to improving this skill. Have your athletes start to lean when they are 1—1.5 metres away from the line, any more than that and they will be limiting their speed over the final few metres of the race.

Getting Started in Track and Field Athletics

What is a dip finish?

The end of a sprinting race is determined when the athlete's torso (i.e. their chest) crosses the line. It is important to tell children that it is not their feet or arms that signals the end of the race.

As the athlete approaches the final two strides of the race they lean forward (dip) so as to extend their chest forward without falling over. To help counter balance this lean, the athlete pushes arms behind their back.

Coaching Tips

Tell your young athletes that the only person whose performance that they can influence is their own. Unless they somehow magically possess some kind of superhero x-ray powers, no amount of hard looking at another athlete will make that athlete slow down.! Try to have your athletes focus on an imaginary tape strung across the finish. Burst the tape!

Getting Started in Track and Field Athletics

What is a photo finish?

Given that races at the highest levels—Olympic Games, World Championships, etc, can only have 100ths of a second separating runners, a means to identify the finishing order was needed. The advent of high speed photography help to revolutionise the judging of track events. As the runners approach the final 5m of the finishing line, the camera takes many photos so that when processed onto long strip of film, it appears that the runners are sprinting in very slow motion. Dead heats—a piece of track jargon that means that two (or possibly more) athletes finished together and could not be separated by the judges— are now a rarity due to photo finish technology.

Questions children will ask:

"Why do some coaches say "run through the tape?"
Before the days of photo finish technology a thin length of "tape" (actually—it was something called Worsted) was held across the finishing line. The first runner across the line would have the tape break across their chest and they would know that they had won the race. The phrase "run through the tape" is simply another way of encouraging an athlete not to slow down before the finishing line.

Getting Started in Track and Field Athletics

The stride of a sprinter

Stride forth ... and may the unknown gloriously unfold before you..

The quality of the sprinter's stride is most critical to the overall performance. Some runners have a stride that eases across the track with grace and composure – indeed, the ancient Greeks honoured style and beauty of movement as much as the race outcome at their Olympic Games. Other athletes appear to strain with every step, their jarring movements limiting the expression of speed. However, if each component of the sprinting action is carefully analysed and developed, even the most ungainly athletes can find improvement.

The stride consists of two parts: **the stance phase** (where the leg is in contact with the ground) and **the flight phase** (where the leg moves through the air and prepares for contact with the ground and the next stride).

The stance phase of sprinting

When the sprinter's foot hits the ground it is only in contact with the track for one tenth of a second. In that short time, all of the mechanical forces of movement must be transferred through the limb and through the foot. The powerful extension of the leg downwards and backwards creates the horizontal movement forward. As the scientist Isaac Newton informed us in his laws of motion: *for every action there is an equal and opposite reaction.* So the action of extending the leg backward also creates a forward and upward movement (the flight phase).

The flight phase of sprinting

As the athlete moves through the air, the limb swings backward and then rapidly forward. It is during this short period that the leg prepares to transfer the momentum. When the front leg hits the ground there can be a braking motion (the speed is inhibited by the contact of the foot with the ground). Good sprinters have learned to efficiently maintain their speed with only the minimum of speed loss through braking movements. Athletes whom have poor techniques may generate lots of speed but lose some of its benefits by jarring stance phase movements.

Getting Started in Track and Field Athletics

When the stride length is too long it can have a braking effect on the transference of speed. Although each athlete has an optimum stride length, there is no magic formula for calculating it. Observations and analysis of the athletes technique and experiential feedback (the athlete is encouraged to experiment with what "feels right" with stride length) will help the athlete arrive at the best stride for them. Limb length, strength of the athlete's muscles, and the state of development of their sprinting technique are key determinants for a coach in advising on stride length.

Key sprinting concepts

Posture — This incorporates the technique of sprinting and the general way that the athlete walks and carries themselves.

Relaxation—an athlete that sprints with relaxed muscles is able to produce faster performances than competing with tense muscles. Build relaxation principles into your program.

Cadence—how fast can the athlete move their legs? There is a physiological and neuro-muscular component that determines leg speed, but this can be enhanced through the games and activities (sprint drills, etc) that are covered over the next few pages.

Trunk stability—The core area (as it is known) is critical for determining posture and application of sprinting power. You can improve core stability through abdominal strength exercises (crunches, modified sit ups, etc), Pilates, and gymnastics.

Balance and rhythm—These skills can be developed if a child has a well balanced sports programme: dance, gymnastics, aerobic exercise, Pilates, etc.

Getting Started in Track and Field Athletics
Sprinting posture

Things to consider in good sprinting technique include:

- Upright torso. Try to avoid exaggerated lean either forward or back. Too much forward lean reduces the movement efficiency of the legs and can place strain on the hamstrings. Excessive backward lean can create muscular tension in the lower back and gluteal (the muscles of the back side) muscles and inhibit sprinting efficiency.

- Have the children work at keeping their fingers and hands relaxed - no clenched fists when they sprint as this creates stiffness and tension in movement. The arm swing should concentrate on the backward swing. Arm carriage should be without excessive tension and be without random jarring movements.

- Core stability – that is strength throughout the abdomen and hips is essential to good sprinting. Good core stability will allow the athlete to raise knees and drive through the back leg (powerful extension of the legs that creates speed).

Getting Started in Track and Field Athletics

Relaxation in Sprinting - Why is it important?

Sprinting is a skill that requires the coordination of a series of complex movement patterns. With races being won by inches, or records being broken by 1/100ths, the efficiency of sprinting skills becomes critical for success. The correct application of technique, the genetic predisposition for a muscle to move fast, psychological factors (motivation, ability to relax, etc) and training effects – how hard does the athlete work - all shape the end result. The emphasis on each element varies according to age. An Olympic sprinter will spend hours rehearsing specific aspects of technique to refine their efficiency. In this book our focus is mainly to create and fun and exciting track and field environment, although preparing young athletes for better performance is only acceptable if the skills are developmentally appropriate and enjoyable. The young athlete is physically unable to cope or adapt to the demands of a training program that emphasizes hard work. At an early age, learning the skills of correct should form the core of the program. Let's start with the principle of relaxation.

A story that I often tell my students is that of a study that was conducted in the 1980's. 40 students— all who were fit but not track athletes—were asked to attend a sprinting session. They were told to run 60m as fast as they could. The next week they returned and were told to again run 60m only on this occasion they were to only run at 80– 90 % of the maximum speed. 38 of the 40 students ran faster running at 80—90 % Why? At top speed the athletes tensed their muscles as they tried to extract every last measure of speed from their body. When they relaxed their muscles worked more efficiently and they—surprisingly—ran faster times. Relaxation is a key principle of fast sprinting. The goal is obviously to run at 100% while being relaxed. Training this quality does not bring immediate results. Just like we don't know that we are a day older but can recognise being a year older, the changes can be imperceptible. Repeated instruction to relax at speed, coupled with video analysis of technique, can enhance relaxation.

Getting Started in Track and Field Athletics

Often, we will do a running session of 6 x 50m fast runs concentrating not on speed but on relaxation. Walk back recovery. Focus on keeping the head still and the muscles and general movements fluid. Athletes are encouraged to identify muscular tension that inhibits fast movement.

A summary of sprinting tips for your athletes

- Run on the balls of your feet
- Concentrate on keeping your head still
- Don't look at your rivals!
- Concentrate on the backswing of the arms
- Relax your hands (don't clench your fists – your arms will become tense if you do!)
- Think about extending your back leg
- Powerfully lift your knees and then extend your leg

Coaching Tips

Run on your toes?

Coaches will often encourage their athletes to run on their toes. This is a misnomer. There is very little strength in the toes themselves and they are unable to generate the forces needed for horizontal propulsion in the stance phase. It is the ball of the foot that absorbs the impact when landing from the flight phase and transfers this momentum into the stance phase. Certainly the phrase "run on your toes" is useful to have children plant their foot in the correct position and not run with flat feet. However "run on the balls of your feet" is a more accurate phrase.

Keep your head still!

Children will often look at others as they race. These head movements create body rotation and shoulder tension and thus reduce performance. Have your athletes practice staring straight ahead and concentrate on their own race. They will likely find that run with improved technique.

Getting Started in Track and Field Athletics

Sprinting technique—Tips for the teacher

- Practise technique work by having your athletes run 40 – 50 fast (but not flat out) while working on some of these tips.

- Only give the runners one or two things to concentrate on during each run.

- Emphasis relaxation on every run.

- Give them full recovery before starting the next run.

- Rest is essential if the full benefit of their practise is to be achieved.

- Fatigue effects skill learning and the athlete may lapse back into the old habits. Young children need to be told when to start their next run by the coach — some will start their next run so that they can state "I was the first to finish the workout."

- If the emphasis is on learning the skills, the control of the pace of the practice is an important classroom management skill.

- Too often they will be concentrating on the outcome of the run rather than the actually skill learning.

- Video tape analysis with instant play back features is a very powerful teaching tool and helps that athletes see how their techniques can change.

Getting Started in Track and Field Athletics

The rules of sprinting

As sprint races are often very close and sometimes only hundredths of second can separate a winner from the rest of the field. Consequently, the rules of this event are strictly applied When an athlete is given a false start it is like a warning that says "we will forgive you this time but don't make that mistake again." There are several ways that an athlete can receive a false start:

- Trying to start before the gun has been fired
- Trying to unsettle a rival through actions — i.e. twitching so that your rival will false start
- Trying to unsettle your rival with words — i.e. trying to break their concentration so that they false start

If an athlete fails to respond to the commands of the race starter in a timely manner they will be awarded one false start — i.e. the athlete cannot delay the start of the race.

How many false starts are your allowed in a sprint race?

On January 1st, 2003 a new rule for starting a sprint race was introduced. There will no longer be one false start allowed for each runner before a disqualification. The new rule states that there will be 1 false start allowed, the next time the gun is fired, the race is on. Anyone who false starts on the second gun will be disqualified at the end of the race.

Some schools and associations will still operate with the old rule – each runner being allowed one false start. It is important to inform the children of the rule as it now exists.

Sometimes a bizarre situation may occur and a false start occurs through no fault of the athlete. The race starter will review the situation and can decide whether to award an athlete the false start or declare the situation a Faulty Start. In a faulty start no-one is to blame. Example : At a national championship the 100m final was getting ready to start. The athletes were called into there "get set" position when suddenly a young child screamed out "GO!" Several of the athletes sprinted out of their starting blocks. The race starter fired the recall gun—one that told the athletes that there had been a false / faulty start. In that example no false start was awarded.

Getting Started in Track and Field Athletics

Other rules of sprinting include:

- **Staying in your lane**

In the 100m the athletes just have to run in a straight line and at the highest levels they seldom run in another lane. If they do, they are disqualified. Up to the 1950's, each lane in the 100m was separated by lengths of string attached to small pegs that were nailed into the track. Thus, this barrier made it difficult for an athlete to sway into an opponents path. In the 200m race—which requires the athlete to run around a bend, it is tempting for an athlete to run close to the edge of their lane and cut some distance. The rules are ruthlessly applied. If you take a step out of your lane, you are disqualified. The exception to this is if you ran out of your lane on the outer section (and thus were running further and not gaining any advantage) - then this infraction would be ignored.

- **Don't interfere with another opponent**

No athlete is allowed to move into the path of another athlete and try to impede their progress. This would include throwing out your arms into the next lane.

- **All athletes must use a crouching start**

No standing starts are allowed.

- **All athletes must use starting blocks**

This ensures that the electronic timing devices — that are attached to the blocks - can be used to prevent any false starting.

- **Wind gauges must be used for a sprinting record to count**

A wind gauge is a device that records the speed of the wind as the athlete races down the track. If the runner had a hurricane force wind behind their back, not surprisingly, they would run much faster than if the wind was in their face. The standard wind speed that is allowed for a record to stand is up to 2 metres per second. A wind speed faster than that will nullify any record that is broken.

Getting Started in Track and Field Athletics

The principles of warming-up

For years, the standard PE warm up activity was the classic "lap around the field." This would allow some elementary children the excuse to demonstrate prowess, or some the opportunity to walk and chat with friends. The warm up can be an integral part of track learning. Our basic format is to raise body temperature through games, follow this with some light stretching and then have the athlete do some strides (fast runs).

Games of tag are just as effective as sustained jogging. Structuring the game's rules so that all kids are active all of the time can prepare the body for the lesson. A simple game is to start with one chaser—wearing a bib— and as soon as you are caught you also become a chaser. The object is to be the last student left. If you play this in a large area, the students can end up sprinting, accelerating, jogging, etc over significant distances.

After a few minutes of games, we carry out our stretching routines. We do a blend of static and dynamic stretches. Although some stretching is advisable, we do not place too much emphasis on this. The children already have good joint range of movement by virtue of their age and lack of significant muscle mass (i.e. they haven't yet gone through puberty). Also, recent evidence suggests that stretching prior to a competition can actually reduce an athlete's power.

A few fast runs (known as strides) e.g. 4 - 6 X 40m that concentrate on speed and relaxation complete the preparation for the start of the skill learning and practise. The strides give the athlete, not only the chance to prepare for themselves for optimum speed, but also review and practise aspects of running skills that have already been taught and hopefully learned.

Getting Started in Track and Field Athletics

Warm up games

The following games are not the specific invention of track. Some are taken from the world of Physical Education and can be easily adapted to the gymnasium or to many other sports. The intent with these games is to get all children immediately active and enjoying a fun game. Children who might be reluctant to run for 5 minutes without stopping will often play a game that fulfills the same purpose.

Tails

This is a very simple game that is effective in warming up the children before a track activity. Each member of the class takes a bib (pinny) and places in their shorts as if they were wearing a tail. The coach should mark out a square with 4 cones and tell the children that they must stay within this area. Each child must run after another and try to pull out the tail of a classmate. If successful the tail is dropped on the ground. The tail-less athlete picks up their tail and starts a new (thus nobody is "out.") You can challenge the children to see how many tails they can catch in a 2 / 3 minute period (you will not want to play this games for much more than 4 minutes).

Team tails

Split your athletes (class) into 2 groups and give them different colours i.e. the red tails vs. the blues. You can play this game in several ways: Ask each athlete to keep count of the number of tails from the other team that they have caught. Add up each teams total and that will determine your winner. Another way (and very popular with the children) is to play elimination team tails. One team tries to eliminate the other team. Stay within the square. If you lose your tail you sit outside the square (and do stretching exercises in preparation for the next activity). Also, if you run outside the square you are out of the game. The team that eliminates all of their opponents from the game wins.

Individual elimination tails

This follows the same rules as with team tails, but each athlete is "on their own."

Getting Started in Track and Field Athletics

Egg timer games

This activity requires you to work with a partner. One athlete sprints up to a cone and back (a distance of 30—40m). The other partner does as many repetitions of an exercise (that you choose) as possible before your partner gets back to the start line. You then change over. Some exercises could include sit—ups, push —ups, if you are in the gym. You could also have the children do sprint drills the only problem is that they sacrifice quality for quantity. The coach would have to watch for this and determine the type of exercise that is appropriate for the age group.

Steal the treasure

Mark out a large square with four cones and divide your class into 4 groups. Each group stands in a corner with 15 bibs (pinnys) or balls, beanbags, etc. On the word "go" all children run to another team's corner to steal a bib and take it back to their "home" corner. A few rules are necessary with this game: each athlete can only steal one bib at a time. Also, you are not allowed to stop someone from stealing your bibs (i.e. no wrestling matches, thank you!). If you make the square very large—50m by 50m—the children will do a lot of running in a 2 minute game. At the end of the 2 minutes, the team that has stolen the most bibs wins. This is a good game for children who may not be very athletic and whom will baulk at the suggestion of doing fast runs for 2 minutes.

Stuck in the mud

This is a game of tag where athletes have to avoid being caught by a specific number of chasers. If you are caught you stand with your feet shoulder width apart and arms up in the arm (like a static jumping jack). Other athletes can set you free by crawling through your legs. This is a simple game that can be played for 2 minutes as part of a warm —up or as a transition activity (i.e. moving from one skill or game to the next).

Getting Started in Track and Field Athletics

Crows and Cranes

This game is very popular with young children and can be used to develop powers of concentration, ability to accelerate and reach top speed. Working with a partner, the athletes stand toe to toe (to make this game more difficult, you can have the athletes stand 2—5 metres apart). You could have all your athletes participate (i.e. you have two lines of athletes toe to toe). Call one line the Crows, call the other line the Cranes. When you call "Crows!" those athletes turn and run to a line 20—40m away (depending on which aspect of their sprinting you wish to develop). The Cranes will try to catch the Crows by running past them. If you are looking to develop pure acceleration, have your athletes only run 20—25m. To develop maximum speed, have them race between 40—50m. Once the crow has reached the "safe line) marked out by 2 cones with an imaginary white line painted between it, both the crows and the cranes return to the start line. As the "caller" you may decide to call Crows again, or Cranes. The Cranes also have a safe line marked out 20—40m away from the start.

A fun addition to this game is to say "if I shout the word Crocodile, (drag out the Cr sound) and you run, you have to do... 5 bum kick sprint drills, or 10 high knees sprint drills, 5 push-ups, etc. This keeps the children both guessing and concentrating "is he going to say Crow, or Crane, or will it be Crocodile?"

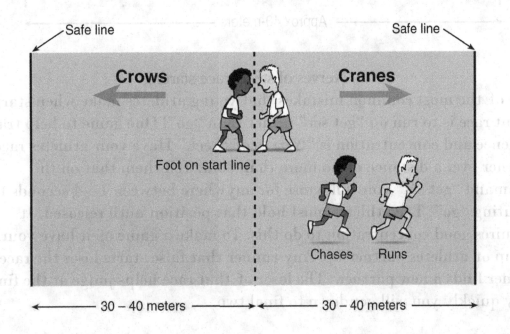

Getting Started in Track and Field Athletics

Turn and run

Another game that develops the athlete's acceleration abilities is turn and Run. One athlete (athlete A) stands about 40m away from their partner (athlete B). The partner (athlete B) is in a crouched start position and waits for their partner to jog toward them. When athlete A crosses a line that is 10m away from B, athlete B sprints past athlete A who is trying to reach a safe line 30 / 40 m away. This can be practiced with both crouched (sprint) and standing start techniques.

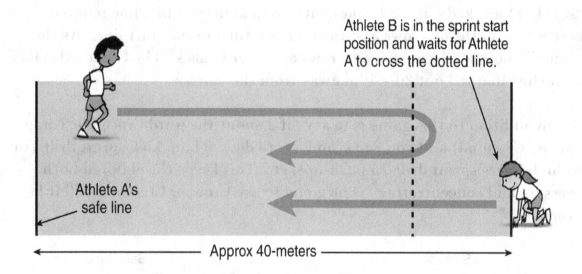

Athlete B is in the sprint start position and waits for Athlete A to cross the dotted line.

Athlete A's safe line

Approx 40-meters

"Nerves of steel" race starting

One of the most common mistakes that young athletes make when starting a sprint race is to run on "get set" rather than "go"! One game to help train patience and concentration is "Nerves of Steel." Have your athletes race a partner over a distance of no more than 30m. Tell them that on the command "get set" you will pause for anywhere between 1—4 seconds before shouting "go"! The athletes must hold that position until released. It requires good concentration to do this. To make a game of it have your group of athletes partner-up. Any runner that false starts loses the race. The winner finds a new partner. The loser of that race helps judge at the finish. Very quickly you will get down to final two.

Getting Started in Track and Field Athletics

Number racing

Split your class into two groups and give them a number so that there are 2 athletes who are number 1, 2 x number 2, 2 x number 3, 2 x number 4, etc. The athletes stand either side of a gym or 20m apart on a field. When you call a number e.g. number 4! Both runners who have that number will race around the track that you have marked out and try to get back to their starting point before their rival. The track is primarily 2 sharp bends with 2 very short straights (and should not exceed 50-60m). You can have several numbers running at the same time and this will help sharpen the children's concentration (e.g., numbers: 4,6, and 8 go!)

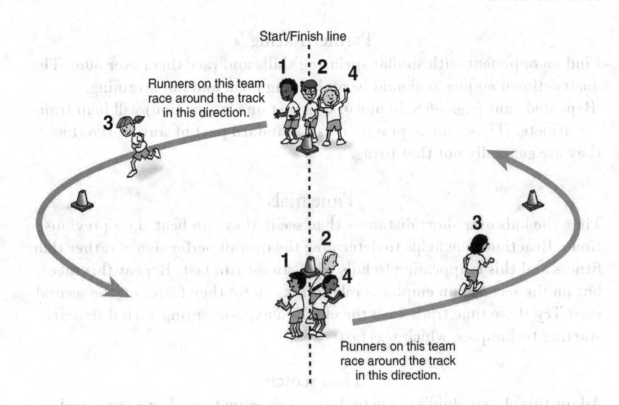

Start/Finish line

Runners on this team race around the track in this direction.

Runners on this team race around the track in this direction.

Getting Started in Track and Field Athletics

Cops and Robbers

One game that we play is titled Cops and Robbers and is a fun way of having the students practise acceleration. Have each student find a partner and have them stand opposite each other about 30m apart. One student—The Robber— tries to sneak up toward the Cop and tag them on their back. The Cop can turn around at anytime and decide whether to chase the Robber to the safe line (30m away). The Cop allows the robber to get as close as possible and then chases. Encourage your students to practise their acceleration and sprinting skills by focusing on sprinting form. If the Cop catches the robber a point is scored. If the robber successfully reaches the cop and tags them on the back, the robber scores a point. Change over roles after several runs.

Partner Racing

Find an opponent with similar sprinting skills and race them over 30m The instructional emphasis should be on holding form and not straining. Repeated runs (e.g.—6 x 30 m working just on acceleration) will help train the athlete. These can be practised as a standard part of any workout as they are generally not that tiring.

Time trials

Time the kids over short distances then see if they can beat their previous time. Reaction time helps to determine the overall performance rather than fitness and this is appealing to kids who cannot run fast. Repeat this race but on the second run emphasis relaxation—were they faster on the second run? Try these time trials with the children experimenting with different starting techniques, which was faster?

Hop scotch

Adapt this classic child's game to develop coordination. Have your students perform it with speed. You can set up a "course" using masking tape on a gym floor.

Getting Started in Track and Field Athletics

Coordination obstacle course

Hop five times, hop other leg, "jump the river" (i.e. across two ropes/ cones), jump to and fro (across the narrow "river") jog to recover then bound, etc — this develops elasticity of the muscles and coordination skills. This could be adapted for use both indoors and out.

Leap frog

I am often amazed at how few of students can actually do a proper leap frog. For many a lack of coordination restricts their success. If it is done properly and the athletes have to jump over a reasonable height, it can develop muscle elasticity which is an important component of sprinting skill.

Elimination Racing

Try this game as a culminating activity. Have your athletes find a partner of similar speed and then form a line with the rest of the class. The athletes then race each other over a very short distance 20—30m. The winner of the race joins the back of the line and has a new partner to race. The loser of the race helps to judge the finishing line. Very quickly the races keep eliminating people until only two are left.

Games Inventory for Sprinting

- Tails / team tails
- Individual / team elimination tails
- Stuck in the mud
- Turn and run
- Cops and robbers
- Number racing
- Steal the treasure
- Nerves of steel
- Crows and cranes
- Leap frog
- Elimination running
- Time trials
- Egg timer races
- Hop scotch
- Coordination obstacle course

Getting Started in Track and Field Athletics

What are Sprint Drills?

These are exercises that are devoted to training specific aspects of the sprinting technique. Each component of sprinting is practiced in isolation through these exercises. As sprinting requires good coordination, these exercises primarily focus on neuromuscular training. For young children, some of these exercises can be difficult, but with sustained practice, huge improvements in the athletes performance can be achieved. The coach will experience a variety of responses from your students— some of them comedic. Don't settle for poor application. Some of these drills will be difficult but they are a staple of the sprinters training program. Insistence on the athlete's best effort can bring improvements and also communicate the message that this is to be taken seriously.

Back ward running is the first drill. The idea here is that the body has a clearly established movement (sprinting) pattern but some of these movements maybe technically very poor. By running backwards for about 20—30m then immediately starting a sprint drill, the theory is that the athlete is confusing the established movement (motor) pattern and then superimposing a new and improved technique for movement. With quality repetition, the new movement pattern becomes established and the athlete has improved performances.

Bum kick drills

This drill trains the backswing of the sprint action. The athletes run slowly and concentrate on kicking their heels against their bum. Some athletes may lean far forward to exaggerate this drill. Encourage your athletes to keep an upright posture.

High knees

This exercise has several benefits: first it can enhance strength and improve the elasticity of the muscles when in the stance position. Students with weak core areas (abdomen and pelvic region) may attempt to compensate for their weakness by leaning backwards in this drill. Have your athletes focus on keeping an upright posture with the knees coming up to a point level with the hip.

High knees with hop

The emphasis on this drill should be on the hop phase which is directed upward rather than horizontally. This drill will combine with benefits of correct knee alignment with power and strength training for the joints and muscles that help create the upward movement. This is quite a difficult skill for young children as it requires good coordination.

Getting Started in Track and Field Athletics

Sample Sprinting Workouts

Grade 2 - 30 minute lesson— Introducing sprint starts

Warm — up
- 3-5 minutes of light jogging,
- 2 running games (e.g. Tails, Crows and Cranes)
- 3 minutes of light stretching. The teacher explains the goals for the lesson.
- 5 x 30 / 40m fast runs—concentrate on good technique

Skill Building
- Introduction of sprint starting
- Demonstration of key principle (using an influential athlete or demonstrate yourself)
- Explain 2 rules
- 5/6 sprint starts over 30m
- Race over 50m

Games to finish
- 2/3 games of tag
- Gentle warm down

Notes:
Build the unit around skills, knowledge, and fun games. The emphasis for this age group should be more on the games than pure skills. Certainly the children will be interested in the sprint drills but they will have limited success with them. Many of the fun games mentioned earlier in this book will give a fun focus to your class. The stories of the sport, knowledge of the rules, and critical thinking skills can be introduced and can inspire and intrigue these eager young minds. If you have PE five days a week, it is recommended that the track unit for grade 2 be delivered 3 times on 5 (every other day would be great).

Competitions? We host 4 fun track meets throughout May and the Grade 2 students are invited. No times are recorded, no finishing places decided, no ribbons awarded—the children run in as many races as we can hold in 1.5 hours. It is lots of fun and 200 boys and girls attend. This is perfect for the Grade 2's.

Getting Started in Track and Field Athletics

Grade 3 - 30 minute lesson— Increasing our knowledge of sprinting

Warm — up
- 5 minutes of light jogging,
- 2 / 3 running games (e.g. Turn and run, stuck in the mud, etc)
- 3 minutes of dynamic stretching. The teacher explains the goals for the lesson.
- 5 x 30 / 40m fast runs—concentrate on good technique

Skill Building
- Introduction of sprint starting biomechanics
- Demonstration of a key principle - What are mistakes commonly made and how do we correct them?
- Explain rules of sprinting
- 5/6 sprint starts over 30m
- Race over 50m

Games to finish
- 2/3 games of tag
- Gentle warm down

Notes:
The Grade 3 age group are ready for more knowledge about this sport and may be able to apply some of the concepts more effectively. As with all the age—groups covered in this book the emphasis is still on fun. Some children will be able to incorporate some of the sprint drills into their techniques— but many will fail. Coordination of movement will still be a challenge for many of these athletes. Fun track meets built on participation, relays and lots of races will prove to be popular for the athletes of this age.

Getting Started in Track and Field Athletics

Grade 4 - 40 minute lesson - Working on maximum speed

Warm — up
- 5 minutes of jogging,
- 2 / 3 running games (e.g. Turn and run, stuck in the mud, tails)
- 5 minutes of dynamic stretching with sprint drills and coordination skills thrown in to add challenge. The teacher explains the goals for the lesson.
- 5 x 30 / 40m fast runs—concentrate on good technique

Skill Building
- Practise sprint starting 4/5 starts over 20m
- Demonstration of a key principle - What are mistakes commonly made and how do we correct them?
- Explanation of the benefits of relaxation in sprinting
- Race over 50m working on maximum speed
- Emphasize relaxation and good form

Games to finish
- 2/3 games of tag
- Gentle warm down

Getting Started in Track and Field Athletics

Grade 5 - 40 minute lesson - Developing Acceleration

Warm — up
- 5 minutes of jogging,
- 2 / 3 running games that emphasize acceleration (e.g. Turn and run, crows and cranes, cops and robbers)
- 5 minutes of dynamic stretching with sprint drills and coordination skills thrown in to add challenge. The teacher explains the goals for the lesson.
- 5 x 30 / 40m fast runs—concentrate on good technique

Skill Building
- Practise sprint starting 4/5 starts over 20m
- Demonstration of principles of acceleration - What are mistakes commonly made and how do we correct them?
- Race over 40m working on acceleration
- Emphasize relaxation and good form

Games to finish
- 2/3 games of tag
- Gentle warm down

Getting Started in Track and Field Athletics

What equipment do I need to be a sprinter?

Unlike many team sports that require an expensive range of clothing and equipment, track and field athletics is accessible to anyone willing to exert the energy to run. With footware, an athlete has 3 options:

- To run barefoot
- To wear running shoes / gym shoes
- To wear spiked track shoes

Some of the great African distance runners have run barefoot in Olympic Games, but this is not advisable for young children. Teachers and coaches should recognize that there are too many liability issues that could arise from injuries (hidden sharp objects in the grass, bee stings, etc) sustained from barefoot running.

Abebe Bikila—the barefoot marathon runner

Abebe Bikila was considered by many to be one of the World's greatest marathon runners. Bikila was a soldier and personal body guard for the King of Ethiopea, Haille Sellaise, and it was expected that he stand on guard duty for two days without a break. His endurance abilities were about to become legendary when he competed in the Rome Olympic Games of 1960. Most marathon runners would wear shoes to protect them from the intense pounding of running 26 miles on the road. Bikila, however, decided to run in the Olympics with bare feet. The ancient streets of Rome with their hard cobbled surfaces and rough roads were no match for the this brilliant Ethiopean runner.

Can you imagine, 26 miles of running with no shoes on!

Getting Started in Track and Field Athletics

Athletic footware is a multi billion dollar industry and slick marketing campaigns will do their best to convince us they we need their shoes to reach the highest levels. I do not counsel parents to buy expensive footware— just footware that is supportive and protective of the young athlete's body. Spiked shoes are an integral part of high performance athletics and there is no doubt that they offer excellent traction on a running track. The metal spikes are located at the front of the shoe's base and are generally 7mm in length. Cross country runners might use 12mm spikes on very muddy courses but spikes of that length would prove to be counter productive on the track.

At what age should an athlete start to wear spikes?
From grade 3 onward, an athlete might like to try wearing spikes, however, gym shoes will serve the same purpose. As the athlete becomes more involved in the sport, the parent might consider buying a pair of spikes.

Getting Started in Track and Field Athletics

Questions children ask..

Are there many different types of running track?

Running tracks may come in many shapes and lengths (some of which are illegal). In the ancient Olympic Games, the track length was 192 m per lap. In today's Olympics, the track length is 400m. For a record performance to count, it must be held on a 400m track. Some school tracks may be of different lengths due to restrictions on space—my university track was pear shaped with a very short bend at the bottom and very long bend at the top; clearly an illegal track. Thus it is difficult to compare the performances of one school athlete with another.

The standard length of an indoor running track is 200m but again there are some that are very short. On one occasion, I ran on track that was 136m per lap—you had to run a lot of laps to complete a mile!

There are essentially 3 different types of running track:
- Grass
- Cinder
- Synthetic (sometimes known as Tartan)

Grass tracks are probably the most common track that a school will use—but they are also not likely to yield the fastest performances. The uneven surfaces preclude optimum performance.

Cinder tracks were the norm before the advent of the synthetic track. Cinders—the ash leftover from coal use— would be rolled in thick layers on the track until they became firm. On a rainy day, however, following another runner would leave you covered with black splatter marks from the cinders.

Getting Started in Track and Field Athletics

Surprisingly, synthetic tracks can vary in speed. Some tracks can be well suited to sprinters and help to produce fast times, while other tracks may be better suited to the distance runners. The thickness of the rubber, and the type of substrate—that is the surface that underlies the rubber i.e. concrete or ashphalt– determine the reaction to the runner's foot hitting the track. A soft bouncy track might suit a distance runner but a firmer track would help the sprinters. Some tracks around the world have the reputation of being a "fast track" as this is often due to its composition.

It is difficult to compare the brilliance of world records that were achieved on different types of running tracks. Synthetic tracks are undoubtedly faster than cinder tracks but the athletes of yester-year did not benefit from the advances in sports science. How would an Olympic Champion from say the 1930's e.g. Jesse Owens, compare with today's fastest athletes if he could use a synthetic track and train using modern methods?

Relay Races

Getting Started in Track and Field Athletics
Relay races

In modern track championships there are two types of sprint relay:

- 4x100m relay (which means there are 4 people on your team with each of them running 100m.)

- 4X 400m relay (this means there are four people on your team with each person running 1 lap of the 400m track)

- Some track meetings will host a medley relay. This event may feature a variety of distances e.g. 2x100m, 1x200, 1x400m, all four runners being a member of the same team. This a very good developmental relay for young children as it gives them the opportunity to race in a relay format over different distances.

Relays are often the last events of a track meet. They are races that require the quick passing of the relay baton (or stick as it is called in America) from one team member to the next. There is a great deal of strategy and risk in the event and surprisingly, the winner is not always the team with the fastest individual runners, sometimes a team with slower individual runners can win because they pass the baton with great speed and momentum.

The relay baton must be exchanged (that is, passed from one team member to the next) within a zone (20m long) that is marked on the track. If you exchange the baton outside of the zone, your team is disqualified. There have been many occasions when a team with the world's fastest sprinters failed to complete the race because they broke this very important rule.

The history of relay racing

There is no evidence that the ancient Greeks had sprint relay races. However, there was an event termed the Lampadedromia where teams of 6—10 runners would race each other over very long distances. Each team carried a flaming torch and this is probably the origin of the modern day Olympic torch relay.

Getting Started in Track and Field Athletics
The rules of 4 x 100m relay racing

- A team must consist of 4 runners.

- The runners in the 4x100m race must stay in their assigned lane for the whole race. If a runner takes a step outside their lane they will be disqualified.

- A team that doesn't exchange the baton with the change zone (20m long) will be disqualified. It is the relay baton that must be taken within the relay zone, so the runner can actually be outside the zone (just) but as long as their hand takes the baton within the zone it is okay.

- The relay baton must be at least 28 cms in length and no more than 30cms.

- An athlete is not allowed to push their teammate at the exchange area and try to give them an advantage.

- A runner is allowed to stand up to 10m before the exchange zone—this is a very important point when a team considers on which stage to place their runners.

Questions children ask
Who makes the rules for track and field athletics?

Track and field athletics is governed by an organization called the International Amateur Athletic Federation (IAAF). The IAAF is responsible for creating the rules and ensuring that they are fair, relevant, and help to keep the sport exciting. The IAAF is also responsible for promoting the sport and every two years, a World Track and Field Championship is held.

Visit the IAAF website: www.IAAF.org

Getting Started in Track and Field Athletics

There are four runners on the sprint relay team and each leg has a specific name that helps describe the role of that athlete: The first runner is known as the first leg or starter. This person may be your athlete whom reacts well to the sound of the gun and can accelerate quickly.

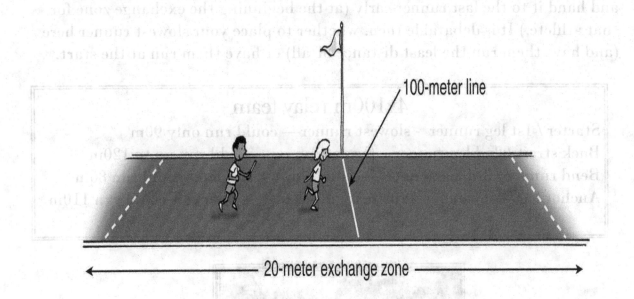

100-meter line

← 20-meter exchange zone →

Some teams may place their slowest runner on the first leg—why? Remember, one of the rules of relay racing states that an athlete may stand up to 10m before the exchange zone and start to accelerate so that when they take the baton, not only are they within the zone but they are also running very fast. With excellent timing (and lots of practice), it is—in theory — possible to have your slowest runner complete only 90m and your fastest runner run 120m. How is 120m possible? The 2nd runner will run the usual 100m plus 10m before the 100m start line. At the 3rd runner's exchange, that runner could stand toward the end of the exchange box thus allowing your fastest runner to add the extra 10m distance to their run. By taking the baton 10m early and giving it 10m late, they have added 20m to their 100m race. A great advantage for the team that places their fastest runner on the 2nd leg!

Getting Started in Track and Field Athletics

The 3rd runner on this relay team should be your athlete that can run around bends the fastest. Some athletes are excellent when running in a straight line but struggle on a curve—it is better tactics, then, to save the fastest runners for the strait and put your 3rd fastest on the top bend. This runner could only run 80m—they could take the relay baton at the end of the exchange zone and hand it to the last runner early (at the beginning the exchange zone for that athlete.) It is debatable then, whether to place your slowest runner here (and have them run the least distance of all) or have them run at the start.

4x100m relay team

Starter / 1st leg runner - slowest runner— could run only 90m
Back strait / 2nd leg runner—fastest runner—could run up to 120m
Bend runner / 3rd leg runner—second slowest runner—could run 80m
Anchor leg / 4th runner—the team's 2nd fastest runner—could run 110m

---

On your marks!

The last leg or anchor often features the team's fastest runner. This always amazes me that the best teams in the world will do that given at the maximum distance the anchor can sprint is 110m as opposed to 120m for the second leg runner. Surely you would want your best runner to run the furthest

Getting Started in Track and Field Athletics

How to exchange the baton

The relay baton must be passed from one team member to another. It cannot be thrown or exchanged in any other way but a pass from hand to hand. There are a number of techniques to exchange the baton: the upward swing where the baton is swept up into the hand and the downward swing onto the flat palm of an outstretched hand (see picture below).

A fast exchange of the relay baton is achieved when the athletes accelerate as the incoming runner passes a mark 10—12m out. If the timing is correct, both runners will be at a good speed and the exchange occurs without a loss of momentum.

Getting Started in Track and Field Athletics

Common mistakes made with relay baton exchanges

- The outgoing runner starts to sprint too soon and the runner with the relay baton fails to catch him (and make the exchange)
- The outgoing runner sprints too soon and runs outside the exchange zone.
- The outgoing runner attempts to correct the mistake by slowing down hoping to stay in the exchange zone. This loss of speed can have a devastating effect on the team's performance.
- The outgoing runner turns back to look for the incoming runner—it is hard (if not impossible) to sprint with your back twisted! Once you have started to sprint, don't look back. Wait for the call to put your hand back from your teammate.
- The incoming runner finds it difficult to place the relay baton in the hand of the outgoing runner because that athlete keeps waving their hand around "searching" for the baton. Keep the hand still and it is an easy "target" for the incoming runner to place the baton in.

Organise your practice so that each child runs each leg

Quite simply: the more relay practice that young children have, the better they will become. It is very hard for the children to overcome the need to look backwards and grab the baton from their partner. With this practice, however, they can learn to trust that the baton will be placed into their hand and then they can concentrate on fast running. Here are several activities that can help promote this trust...

Getting Started in Track and Field Athletics

Stand and grab

Have your athletes find a partner. The athletes stand one behind the other and at arms length apart. The runner who will receive the relay baton swings their arms as if they were running (but they do not move off the spot). The runner behind carries the relay baton and also pretends to be running and swings their arms in a typical running action. The athlete at the front never looks back. When the athlete with the baton shouts "hand," the front runner puts their hand down and grabs the baton. Practise this several times. Make sure the athlete giving the baton knows which hand the receiving athlete will put down.

Up and Back relay

Have your students run an "Up and Back" relay for their first introduction to this race. They will get a feel for holding the baton and this can be a fun game to play in teams. Emphasise some of the rules of relay racing: Specifically, you are not allowed to throw the baton to your teammate!

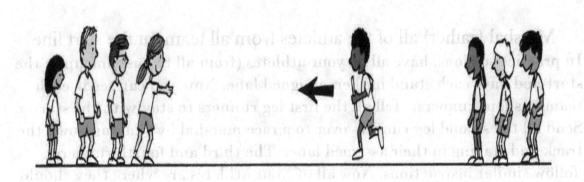

Getting Started in Track and Field Athletics

Move to the next leg

The children on your relay team should all be given the opportunity to try each of the stages of the race. One way to do this is to instruct the team to run their leg—then they are told to *"stay where they are"* and get ready to start another race i.e. the 1st runner will then become the second leg runner, the 2 nd leg runner becomes the third, the third runner moves to the last leg, and the last leg runner starts the next race. After 4 races, the athlete has run each of the legs of this relay. Make sure that the athletes are given a good rest between each run.

Common mistakes in organizing relay races

On a 6—8 lane running track, there are many painted lines and this can be very confusing for a young athlete. If you tell them that they are the 3rd runner in lane 5 (and 2nd heat) many will completely forget where they are supposed to be. Mistakes are invariably made and some teams will not complete the race because their athlete was in the wrong place. Here are some suggestions that will help a coach / teacher marshal the athletes and get them to their correct place on the track.

Marshal (gather) all of the athletes from all teams at the start line

In practice sessions, have all of your athletes (from all teams) line up at the start and have each stand in their assigned lane. Now you can see if each team has four runners. Tell all the first leg runners to stay with the starter. Send all the second leg runners over to a race marshal by running down the track and staying in their assigned lane. The third and fourth runners follow similar instructions. Now all of your athletes are where they should be and the race can begin.

In a track meet where there are hundreds of athletes, marshalling for the relays can be a nightmare that results in the event falling way behind schedule. Rather than marshalling the athletes at one spot and then sending them off, have all of the athletes in all races go to their designated leg, e.g. *"would all last leg runners go to the top of the track, would all third leg runners go to the top bend, etc."* Have 4 well trained marshals who each have a clipboard with race by race lane assignments (i.e. photocopy your heat sheets 4 times so each marshal reads the sheet race by race and has the athletes lining up in the correct lane. A well trained marshal will have all 3rd leg runners for several races in advance, sitting down in lane order waiting for the race before them to finish.

Teachers Corner

Children will often get confused by the number of lanes on the track. Tell your athletes that the lanes are always numbered from the inside of the track out. So, if they have no idea which is lane number 5, stand on the grass on the infield and start to walk across the track. Count each lane that you cross until you reach 5. If the athletes are confused by their leg number and lane number, give them the leg descriptor rather than a number: e.g. *"You are the anchor runner on the 5th lane. Or, you are the back strait runner in lane 2,"*etc. Pointing to the general direction will also help these children confused by numbers.

Questions children ask

"Why do athletes in relay races get head starts?"

It is important to remind the children that the running track is only 400m around in lane 1. In each subsequent lane, the track is: Lane 2 — 407m, Lane 3 — 414m, Lane 4 — 421m, Lane 5 - 428m, etc(7m extra per lane). This extra distance is because the track has two bends. When the children are assigned to their lanes, each runner will be placed 7m metres in front of the runner behind them—this "staggered start" as it is known ensures that each team runs the 400m.

Getting Started in Track and Field Athletics
The World Records

The World record for the 4 x100m relay for men is currently 37.40 seconds set in 1993 by the United States of America national team.

The World record for the 4 x 100m relay for women is currently 41.37 seconds set in in 1985 by the German Democratic Republic national team.

How do you set a world record?

The answer to this question is not as simple as it first seems. For a world record to be accepted a number of very strict—but common sense—conditions must be met:

- The track must be certified as being as being accurate to within 1/10th cms. If it is not accurate, over several laps (a 10,000m race has 28 laps of the track) the athlete could end up running significantly less than the required distance.

- For a sprint record to count, the race must be held with a following wind that is less than 2m / second. If it exceeds this speed, it will give the runner an unfair advantage compared to an athlete who ran with no wind behind them.

- The record claim can only be submitted if the performance was timed using an electronic timer, and the track meet was using highly qualified officials. For instance, a record claim would not be accepted if a few of your friends got together at the track and timed you with a wrist watch! If all conditions are met, a committee of the International Amateur Athletics Federation (IAAF) will meet and consider if this record is legitimate. Many record claims have been rejected because they either broke rules, or could not be verified. As late as the 1970's, records were rejected because the race had a pacemaker (or rabbit as they are some times called) - this practice is now commonplace.

Getting Started in Track and Field Athletics

- What is the difference between a world best and world record? Some events—like the marathon and race walking, are held on courses that may have lots of hills or lengthy sections of downhill running. As no two courses could be exactly the same over 26.2 miles, the fastest performance in the world is called a world best rather a world record.

The 4 x 400m Relay

The 4 x400m relay is, usually, the very last event of a track meet. It is an exciting race with each member of a team running one full lap of the 400m track. Some of the rules of this relay are very different to the sprint relay (4x100m). In the long relay—as it is sometimes called—the first runner must run the lap and stay in their assigned lane; they are not allowed to leave that lane at any time. If they do run outside of the lane—even just a few steps—the team is disqualified. At the end of the first lap, the athlete passes the baton to the second runner whom must also run in the assigned lane. The big difference with the second leg is that all runners can cut into lane 1 (the one closest to the grass in-field) after they have run 100m of their leg (500m into the race). A white line is painted on the track to help these 2nd leg runners know when it is safe to cut to the inside. The 3rd and 4th (last) leg runners are allowed to run in any lane (although lane 1 is the shortest distance around the track). The lead often changes in this race and it is an exciting spectacle to see some of the world's great 1 lap sprinters battle it out.

Questions Parents Ask..

Should young children run the 4 x 400m relay?

Children who attempt to sprint for 1 lap (400m) will quickly need to utilize their anaerobic energy source. As this energy system is poorly developed in young children, the likelihood is that these athletes will rapidly fatigue and not be able to complete the distance at a good speed. The 4X 400m relay—and 400m races—is more suitable for teenagers who can draw on their developing anaerobic system to help them through this race.

Getting Started in Track and Field Athletics

World records for the 4X400m relay

The men's world record is
2minutes 54.2 seconds set in 1994
by the United States of America
national team.

The women's world record is
3 minutes 15.17 seconds set by the
former Soviet Union in 1988.

Distance running

"Swiftness of foot is one of the most highly prized qualities a man may possess"

- Xenophanes — Greek Philosopher

Getting Started in Track and Field Athletics

The history of distance running

The great distance runners in ancient history tended to be messengers. As there were no easy means to get a message from one place to another, kings, generals and politicians came to rely on slaves or soldiers to carry their words to another. Perhaps one of the most famous messengers was a Greek (Spartan) soldier named Pheidippides. In 490 BC the Persian (today known as the country of Iran) King, Darius, invaded Greece with an army of 20,000 men. The Athenian army battled the Persians at the town of Marathona but were outnumbered 2:1. Realising that help would be needed, Pheidippides was dispatched to Sparta. Pheidippides was known as a Hemerodromoi, an warrior specifically trained to run very long distances—presumably to carry messages. Athens to Sparta was a distance of 229km which—it is claimed—that Pheidippides covered in 24hours. The Spartans were too busy celebrating a religious festival to send an army however. The battle raged on and the Athenians prevailed (killing 6,500 Persians while only losing 192 of their own men). With the battle won, Pheidippides was told to inform the King who was in Athens—a distance of 40km—of their victory. The story goes that an exhausted Pheidippides staggered into the King's palace and declared *"Nenikhkamen—we have won,"* after which, he died from exhaustion. It is a popular misconception that the ancient Greeks held long distance races—such as the marathon. All of the races were in held in the stadium and the kings believed that exhausted runners displayed no beauty in their running.

When the ancient Olympic Games were resurrected in 1896 by Baron Pierre De Coubertin, a long distance race was held. The name Marathon to describe the run. The distance between Marathona and Athens is now the trademark distance(42 km or 26.2 miles) for this race. Fittingly, the Greek athlete Spiridon Louis won the first modern Olympic marathon race.

Getting Started in Track and Field Athletics
Why is the Olympic marathon distance 26.2 miles?

When the London Olympic Games of 1908 were held, it was decided that the race would start at the King's home—Windsor Castle — and then run to the stadium in the centre of London, a distance of 26miles. The finishing line for this race was, however, on the opposite side of the track to where the King and Queen of England were sitting. The Queen spoke to the organizers and had them add point 2 of a mile to the race distance so that it finished directly in front of the King and Queen. Even to this day, marathon races all over the world are 26.2miles.

The loneliness of the (Greek) long distance runner!

Not all Greek athletes were brilliant runners. Nikarchos, a poet (and presumably a man with a sharp wit) wrote a letter to a friend describing the abilities of an unfortunate athlete: " Charmos, a long distance runner finished 7th in a field of 6. A friend ran along side him shouting "keep going, Charmos." and although fully dressed, beat him. And if he had had five friends he would have finished 12th."

Is there a place for the likes of Charmos in a track team? Most certainly yes— school teams are full of kids like Charmos, in fact this book has been written for people like him!

Captain Barclay's Run

Captain Robert Barclay is a name that is probably unknown to most people, but if you had lived in 1803 – Georgian England – his name was on the lips of every gambling man and every sports enthusiast. The name Barclay is synonymous with one of the greatest athletic feats of endurance of all time. Captain Barclay was an unusual man: slight in stature but possessing an iron will that helped complete unimaginable feats of distance running and walking. One such challenge was to see if he could run 1 mile every hour for 1 thousand hours (40 days and nights!) He was allowed to rest whatever time he had left within the hour; e.g. a 10 minute mile allowed him to rest for 50 minutes. As the challenge progressed his miles became slower to the point where he was not taking any rest all. In today's money there was almost $30 million in gambling bets resting on Barclay's run. Amazingly, Barclay completed this run and then promptly slept solidly for 3 days!

Getting Started in Track and Field Athletics

The World Records of middle distance running

For many years observers in the sport of middle distance running felt that running one mile in less that four minutes was impossible. This was one of the great barriers in physical capacity—something a human would not breach. By 1954 **Roger Bannister** — an English university student— had changed the way the sporting world would view these "barriers." Running 3minutes 59.4 seconds, Roger Bannister had placed his name in the record books—the first human to run under 4 minutes for a mile. Almost 20years later **John Walker** from New Zealand had broken yet another barrier: 3minutes 50 seconds for a mile, when he ran 3:49.4 seconds.

Records are made to be broken is the famous running cliche; how low can this record go? Will we see a sub 3minute 40 second mile?

The current record is .. 3minutes 43.19 seconds by the Morrocan athlete **Hicham El Gueroujj**.

The World Records

800m men Wilson Kipketer—Denmark 1min 41.11

800m women Jarmila Kratochvilova—Czechoslovakia 1min 53.28

1500m men Hicham El Guerrouj Morroco 3mins 26.00

1500m women Qu Yunxia China 3mins 50.46

5000m men Kenenisa Bekele Ethiopea 12mins 37.35

5000m women Jian Bo China 14mins 28.09

Getting Started in Track and Field Athletics
What is the difference between middle and long distance running?

Middle distance races are have traditionally included the 800m and 1500m races. These races are held on the track and require the athlete to have great speed and the ability to sustain that pace for a long way. Many athletes will run too fast too soon and will not be able to complete the race at such a fast pace. Thus, the tactics of a middle distance require excellent pace judgement.

Long distance races on the track include the 3000m, 5000m, and 10,000m. Today's world class athletes not only have excellent endurance, but they are also able to sprint incredibly fast at the end of a long race. Even the marathon race— 42 km long—has seen some sprint finishes at the end.

Getting Started in Track and Field Athletics
The science of distance running

For an athlete—of any age—to run for a sustained period they will need energy. The body can create this energy in a number of different ways:

- Alactic Anaerobic system
- Aerobic energy system
- Anaerobic energy system

What follows is a basic primer in exercise physiology, some knowledge of these energy systems is needed as it will help teachers and coaches understand how some activities are within the developmental range or limitations of young athletes participating in track and field athletics.

Each cell in the human body needs a chemical called Adenosine Triphosphate (ATP) to create energy— the process is very complex and is beyond the scope of this book to cover it in detail.

Exercise physiology: The Bear Necessities

Imagine this scenario: You are walking through the forest when out jumps a very hungry black Bear. You decide to run (perhaps not the best strategy but you don't fancy being today's main course!) The first energy system to create ATP to help you escape from the bear is called the **Alactic Aanerobic System**. This system can provide a rich burst of energy and does so without using oxygen. This system, however, is exhausted after only a few seconds (4-6).

The bear is rapidly bounding after you snapping its jaws and barking "yum, yum." You need more energy quickly. The body recognizes this need and switches to the **Anaerobic Energy System** which is a rich source energy created in cells without the need for oxygen. You are running as fast as you can but start to feel your muscles become tight. This fatiguing of the muscles is due to the production of lactic acid—a very unfortunate side effect of the anaerobic energy system. Your body is unable to sustain this very high rate of energy production without oxygen. Fortunately the bear catches the smell of fresh salmon swimming in a nearby stream and loses interest in you.

Getting Started in Track and Field Athletics

You start to slow down but still need to keep running away from the bear. The body now switches to the **Aerobic Energy System**. Depending on your endurance capacity, strength and motivation this system can provide energy for hours (witness the energy demands of marathon running).

This story is from a personal interaction with a huge black bear 3 years ago. While the exercise physiology responses to stress were not foremost on mind as I sprinted across the forest floor, on reflection it was interesting to see how my body switched from system to system.

The bear went hungry—it was the best run of my life!

The children for whom this book is written have poorly developed anaerobic energy systems. It is not until teenage years that this system starts to develop and become a meaningful source of energy. Thus the training emphasis should be on developing the aerobic energy system. Activities that promote this are covered throughout the book.

The Teacher's Corner

Some exercise scientists wanted to determine the effects of different kinds of training programs on sprint endurance in young children. The children were placed into three groups, one group did purely speed training for 20 minutes four times a week. The second group did endurance training for the same amount of time. A third group of children were not given any exercise programs at all.

The aerobic and anaerobic energy systems of the children in each of the groups were assessed. As you would expect, the children in the third group (no exercise) did not improve their fitness levels. The children in both the sprint and endurance groups improved their fitness equally. The implication is that any form of training in young children will help to improve fitness measures. This powerfully supports the view that providing specialized training at any early age only brings a general fitness response.

Dykstra, et al. (1996) Medicine and Science in Exercise and Sport.

Getting Started in Track and Field Athletics

How to train young children in distance running

In an earlier section of this book ingredients of success were considered. Among these, inspiration and motivation play an influential role in young developing athletes. The dictionary describes inspiration as "the action of moving intellect or emotions." By inspiring your athletes you may hope to:

- Help the nervous find courage
- Draw out confidence from the unsure athlete
- Give purpose to the athlete with a wavering commitment
- Push a talented athlete down a path that leads to great success

Whatever the goal that drives your inspirational techniques, coaches must know their athletes and understand how that athlete responds to certain styles of coaching. Using stories can be a powerful way to inspire these athletes. Show casing the talents of children that exemplify a particular skill or virtue is also another way to inspire your athletes. The positive effects of role modeling the behaviour and how this can inspire young athletes is well documented.

Techniques to motivate your distance runners

Some athletes are compelled to practise hard, are very competitive and display an urgent need to succeed. They may run to prove a point, to beat a determined rival, or run just for the satisfaction that running can bring. Psychology has labelled such runners as **Intrinsically Motivated**—their reason to complete this action comes from an internal desire. Athletes who only run because they receive a reward—money, ribbons, a house point, are said to be **Extrinsically Motivated.** Understanding the sources of human motivation and how it can be manipulated to gain an advantage, has been the source of vast numbers of business books and sports psychology research (to name but a few fields). On the next few pages, you will find a number of techniques—some that promote intrinsic motivation, some that rely on rewards to bring the best out of your athletes. Carefully consider which technique might suit the personality profile of your athlete; the underachieving un-fit athlete might better respond with some reward system that recognises the effort that has made (as the athlete knows they will probably never win a race). The high-flying successful athlete might better suit techniques that focus on developing intrinsic motivation— e.g. setting tough personal goals.

Getting Started in Track and Field Athletics

Goal setting and track and field

The benefits of goal setting are well documented in sports psychology. Athletes who set a specific goal are more likely to reach their best performance than an athlete who has stated "I'll just see what happens." There are some key principles in athlete goal setting that may help your athletes structure the way that they prepare for an event:

• **Set effort goals rather than outcome goals**. This is a very important consideration for young athletes. They can only control the amount of effort that they put into the race (sports event) they cannot control the outcome. I often tell my athletes *"We can't change the weather, we can't change how fast the other runners can sprint, the only things we can control is our effort and our attitude. Let's go out there, give our best effort and have fun; the result will take care of itself."* Of course, the desired purpose of the race is to win and to give your best effort to try and reach this goal. For the vast majority of children, this goal is quite simply unattainable, and rather than building them up emotionally for certain disappointment, the coach / teacher can train the athlete to appraise their performance in different ways.

• **Focus on technique and things your athletes can master.** Children who are not very athletic or likely to achieve success (in terms of winning) will look for fun and skill mastery as their sources of motivation. Never assume that the child who is slowly plodding around the track is any less interested in their final time than winners.

• **How do you measure improvement?** It is easy to motivate the successful athlete, the ones who win the ribbons and plot their next victory. It is the athlete who keeps supporting the team (despite an apparent lack of talent) that I particularly want to encourage. A child's sensitivity to remarks is sometimes exploited by bullies to make that child vulnerable. However, this same sensitivity and perceptiveness can be used by a teacher and coach to help subtley build the confidence of the athlete. I will position myself within earshot of an athlete that needs a bit of a boost and say to their parent *"I was really pleased with the effort that Mary has made. I can tell she is working hard and it is great to have her on the team"*, etc. I pretend that I don't know that the athlete is listening. When the athlete goes home that night, the coaches comments are resonating with excitement in the child's mind.

Getting Started in Track and Field Athletics

- **Looking for positives in each race and practise session.** Confidence in young athletes is a quality that is built incrementally. Some athletes will require lots of reassurance, while a few may be suffering from "high self esteem"! Giving each athlete some meaningful information about their performance will help this process.

Throughout this book you will note that I believe children should be introduced to the technical knowledge that leads to a good sports performance. By training the children to analyse their own performance they will be in a better position to utilise your coaching feedback; thus, you can avoid the glib clichés that blight sports coaching and give the children something meaningful that they can actually use.

Getting Started in Track and Field Athletics

Pyramid of Achievement

This can be used to motivate your young athletes to attend regular practices, learn how to apply the skills they have been taught, and analyse their performances. You can design this chart to emphasise areas that you would like to develop—if an athlete achieves all levels of the pyramid, you may choose to give them some sort of reward. The example below is for distance running:

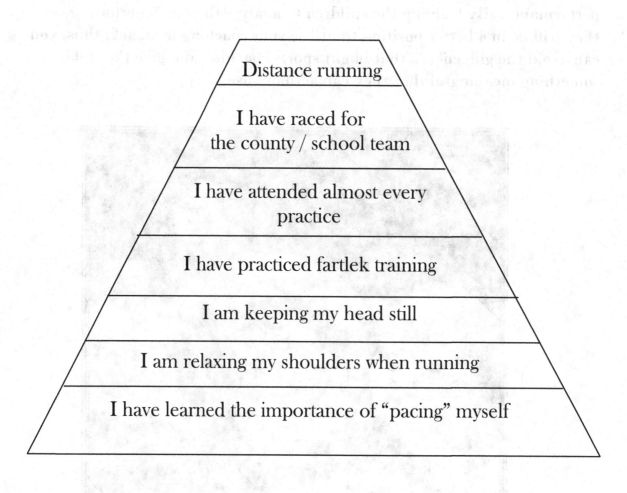

Distance running

I have raced for
the county / school team

I have attended almost every
practice

I have practiced fartlek training

I am keeping my head still

I am relaxing my shoulders when running

I have learned the importance of "pacing" myself

Getting Started in Track and Field Athletics

Training methods

One of the key questions for consideration is how much practise / training should a young child do? What are the benefits of training (if any) and what are the risks? Our society has structured many competitions for young kids with a heavy emphasis on winning – a World Baseball Series for children! Some parents and coaches are pushing kids to improve performance with the message that it is hard work that will get results. Is this appropriate or even true? I would like to start with a review of some of the principles that when correctly applied, can improve fitness. What are the key considerations when designing a training program?

- Frequency of practise
- Duration
- Intensity
- Specificity
- Progression

Frequency: How often do you practise? Obviously, practising 4 times a week will produce better results than only practising once a week.

How much practise is appropriate for an 8 year old child?

If a school offers daily physical education then that should probably be enough. This assumes that the child is active in the class for at least 30 minutes and is developing fitness with challenging aerobic activity (and not spending most of their time warming the benches). If you add healthy active exercise during recess times, the student will develop their fitness without risks of being over extended with a heavy training load. Some children may be able to cope with more practise, others will struggle with their classes – that is where the art and not the science of coaching and teaching comes into play.

Getting Started in Track and Field Athletics

Recommendation for training frequency: Grade 2 – 4 times per week. Grade 3 - 5 times per week. Grade 4 and 5 – 6 times per week (this includes Phys. Ed classes)

Duration: This principle of practise refers to the length of time that the athlete is actively involved in exercise. How long can the young child work? Children have run marathons – at immense risk to their joint health and seldom achieve success as teenagers or adults. Thus some parents / coaches may argue that the child can "run forever." The majority of elementary children will, however, not be able – or motivated enough – to sustain exercise and its discomforts – for more than a few minutes. The challenge for the coach is to structure an endurance activity in such a way that the duration of activity increases to the point where the athlete can gain benefit but is not so long as to be counterproductive.

Recommendations for exercise duration (endurance activity)

Grade 2 – A 20 minute lesson that features 10 minutes of tag games, swiftly followed by 5 minutes of sustained distance running – then a few more games.

Grade 3 – 10 minutes of tag games for a warm up followed by 6 minutes of fartlek running or sustained running. Fartlek is running that combines varying speeds and walking over different distances.

Grade 4 and 5 – 10 minutes tag games for a warm up followed by 8 minutes of sustained running. Can they do more? Yes, however – the coach needs to discern which athletes can cope and for which students will find it demoralizing.

Note: A 25% increase or decrease in these recommendations is possible for capable or challenged kids. The warm up games of tag are a good way of getting all kids working their lungs.

Getting Started in Track and Field Athletics

Specificity: As teenagers and adults our bodies can make specific adaptations to an exercise stimulus. For example, training that works the anaerobic energy system will create improvements in that energy system's efficiency. However, paediatric exercise research has shown that children, it seems, do not make specific physiological adaptations to exercise – their fitness improvements tend to be general. Anaerobic training (as difficult and challenging as it is for young children) will not make a specific improvement but more a general response. The coach would be well advised to avoid that type of training. Being active, whether it is during recess, in Phys Ed classes playing soccer or doing general endurance is just as valuable in improving fitness.

Recommendation for all grades 2 – 5 : Don't structure your practises for specific energy system or fitness responses – they don't occur. Build your practises around the knowledge that the fitness response is general.

The Russian exercise scientist Yakovlev has written three laws that he suggests should govern the way our athletic programs are designed. The first law he titles the **law of overload**. For an athlete's fitness to adapt, it must be challenged—or overloaded. Yakovlev suggested that the initial response to this training is fatiguing, followed by a recovery period. The body then adapts to this challenge (or exercise stimulus) and boosts the fitness level above its previous level (over compensation as Yakovlev describes it). For continued improvements, the exercise stimulus should be delivered at the peak of the over compensation. Thus it should be possible for the athlete to avoid a plateau –or levelling—in fitness improvements. When athletes fail to give themselves the appropriate degree of rest, they are exposed to risks for injury or illness.

If you can fill the unforgiving minute
With 60 seconds worth of distance run,
Yours is the Earth and everything in it,
And—which is more—you'll be a Man, my son!

Rudyard Kipling

Getting Started in Track and Field Athletics

The second principle is the **law of reversibility**. This states that when the exercise stimulus is removed the body has no need to adapt and will start to revert back to its basic level, i.e. a baseline level of fitness.

The third principle Yakovlev considered was the **law of specificity**—this has already been discussed.

Intensity: For the body to make a significant fitness adaptation to exercise, the exercise must be conducted with a degree of intensity. If you make the same effort week in, week out, the body will initially adapt and then plateau – i.e. fitness will neither increase nor decrease. In order to improve fitness the principles previously mentioned must be adjusted in ways that continually challenge the body to adapt. Thus with careful planning, it is possible for fitness to reach very high levels. I use the phrase 'what was once difficult becomes easy with fitness gains." Conversely, a lack of practise can reduce fitness levels (quite quickly!)

So, what degree of intensity should be applied to children's exercise programs? Again, we have to come back to the recognition that a child's fitness response is only at a general level. Children often work within their comfort zone and only a few truly extend themselves to really challenge their capabilities. Inspire and motivate your students to face exercise discomfort not as something to be feared but something to accept, even embraced.

What distances should young children race?

Beyond the recommendations just made, some comment about the distances that children in primary grades should run is needed. Distances of 800m and, at the most, 1km are acceptable. Some coaches will undoubtedly argue that they have athletes who are capable of running much further—why hold these athletes back? I know of children who have run 10km races and even marathons—yes they completed the race—much to the admiration of their parents—but at what risk? The deleterious of long distance running on the child's growth plates are well documented in pediatric medicine. As young children continually place physical stresses in their knee joints they may leave themselves prone to Osgood Schlatters disease— an inflammatory condition that takes long periods of rest to ensure joint recovery.

Getting Started in Track and Field Athletics

The technique of good distance running

Two of the key principles for good distance running (no matter what your age) are efficiency and tolerance. The athlete must be sufficiently conditioned (trained) to tolerate the demands of the run. These may include heat stresses – exercising hard raises the athlete's body temperature (thus they sweat to help dissipate this heat). A fit athlete will have improved thermo-regulation over an unfit runner. An athlete that lacks good conditioning will experience muscular stress e.g. excessive soreness as the muscles are expected to do something that they may not be used to.

Efficient movement can help to improve an athlete's performance – or, conversely, drain their energy with wasteful body movements. As was discussed in the sprinting section of this book, relaxation while running at speed, is essential for the athlete to compete to their highest level. Let's examine the principles of distance running technique, these include:

- **Good posture** - You may hear a coach shout to their athlete "run tall." An athlete with a slouched posture places restrictions on their limbs abilities to move freely. While good posture is essential, make sure that your athletes do not become rigid as they strive for this position. Rigidity leads to muscular tension which, in turn, inhibits performance.

- **Keep the head still** — As the head is the heaviest part of our body, unnecessary movements can waste energy but also create a cascade effect of tension throughout the body; e.g. head wobble creates tension in the shoulders, which might cause a swaying motion in the torso as it tries to correct this tension. Maintaining head position is also a valuable skill for young athletes to learn as it encourages concentration (rather than having them spend time looking over to see how their rivals are doing).

- **Drop the shoulders** — Shoulder tension is very common in young athletes. Their attempts to run ever faster causes them to "shrug" their shoulders up into their necks and this limits their arms ability to swing freely.

Getting Started in Track and Field Athletics

- **Don't paddle the arms** — Many young athletes will develop—unless taught correctly—unusual arm running actions. Some arms will be swung with a paddling action, some may use their arms like a dog pawing, others may develop an arm swing more appropriate for the Church Bell Ringing Club! The arms should swing loosely backward and forward. Have your athletes concentrate on the back swing by pushing their back as far as is comfortable. With the forward arm swing, the arms should reach a mark level with the chest (note that sprinters swing their arms to almost chin level, while marathon runners swing their arms barely higher than stomach level).

- **Keep the torso still**—The strength of your athlete's abdomen (also known as the core area) is very important if the athlete is to reach an efficient level of athletic performance. The core area provides stability to the torso and this limits wasteful body movements (i.e. twisting and turning rotations). As many of the muscles that generate movement have their origin in the core area, good conditioning can help the athlete produce good speed and cope better with endurance. This conditioning can be acquired throughout gymnastics, Pilates, dance, natural play on climbing apparatus, and exercises such as crunches / sit-ups, etc.

- **Concentrate on good foot placement** — Correct foot placement is important to develop as this will help the athlete transfer the forces generated by muscular contraction into forward movement. If an athlete is flat footed, or places their foot with outward (pronation) or inward bias (supination) their body is forced into making compensatory movements in their gait to correct this problem. Over a course of time, injuries can occur. If your athlete does seem to have an unusual gait, it is worth seeking advice from a biomechanics expert or podiatrist.

Questions Parents Ask

Are the difficulties my child is having with these movement patterns just the normal reflections of a child's developmental stages?

Some children are your "natural" runners; they have excellent coordination and run with the grace of a gazelle. Other children— generally those with poor coordination, immature muscle tone, and inadequate physical conditioning — will struggle to acquire an efficient running technique. The first section of this book discussed the importance of children developing certain skills during critical periods of their development. Coordination plays such an important role in many sports that any activity that a child decides to pursue should be rich with opportunities to develop these skills. If a coach takes the time to help correct some of the mistakes that children often make when running, it will serve these children well as they start to specialise in a particular sport in their teenage or adult years. Trying to remediate a biomechanical problem is a lot more difficult once that movement pattern has been established.

Getting Started in Track and Field Athletics

The stride of a distance runner

Is the stride of a distance runner different from that of a sprinter? There are a few key differences that separate the techniques of these two track events. A sprinter is looking to generate the maximum amount of power (and thus speed) possible. The distance runner is looking to run at the fastest speed that they can sustain for the duration of the run. Conservation of energy and stride efficiency are the hallmarks of a good distance running technique. Let's look at some of the principles and consider the most common mistakes that are made.

- Economy
- Relaxation
- Strength
- Flow
- Weight of feet on ground

Economy of the stride refers to the length and ease with which the athletes moves. Athletes who run with exaggerated strides—believing that this will somehow help them to finish the race faster—will tire quicker than an athlete with a good stride length. Under—striding — lots of little pitter-patter steps but going no-where, is also very inefficient. Finding the correct stride length is an experiential process for the athletes, by this I mean that the athlete can learn to recognize the comfort of a good stride by experimenting with the feel of over and under striding. Having your athletes practice runs of 50—60m with the sole purpose of working on their technique and refining their stride will be most valuable.

An economic stride length tries to extract the maximum amount of return for the minimum amount of effort; relaxation is thus, a key feature of good running. If you ever have the opportunity to see world class athletics live, you will be stunned at the beauty and ease with which these distance runners move. They make their event look effortless as they glide through lap after lap like a well oiled machine. The lack of tension in their stride is a result of hours of relaxed running (don't confuse that with making no effort—these runners are going flat out but are doing so with economy).

Getting Started in Track and Field Athletics

How to run a distance race

The start of a distance race has very different commands to that of a sprinting race. The race starter will ask all of the athletes to stand back several metres from the start line and wait for his commands (instructions). When the starter is satisfied that the race can begin he/she will state *"on your marks!"* All athletes must advance to the start line and make sure that their toes are completely behind the line. Once all the runners are still, the starter fires the gun. *Note: there is no "get set!" command in a distance race.*

The tactics of a distance running

Some athletes prefer to follow the leader (known in sports jargon as "sitting") and then waiting to sprint past the leader at the end (also known as "kicking"). Other athletes are unabashed front runners wanting no company in their race. There are some athletes who will choose to execute a sustained surge to the finish line hoping to take the away the finishing speed of the sprinters. A few simply hope that they can hang onto the pace long enough to stay in the race. The perfect race can sometimes be an elusive cocktail of fitness and strategy. Correctly blended, and the performance can be truly memorable. Get one of those elements wrong and its bitter taste lingers. Never is the "recipe" the same for each race. The coach will need to help the athlete formulate a race plan, not only in anticipation of a rival's plan, but also in consideration of the weather, the course and distance. We all know athletes who had the fitness to win a particular race and yet made poor tactical decisions and underachieved. Keeping to a strict tactical plan requires faith in its design, patience in its execution and an unwavering commitment to see it through until the end. When an opponent races off far into the distance the seeds of self-doubt can easily undermine an athlete's plan. The successful athlete rises above this and stays confident that their plan will work.

Race Tactics

- Front running
- Sitting and Kicking
- Surging throughout the race to try and drop a rival
- Running faster over certain parts of the race and easing off at other parts

Getting Started in Track and Field Athletics

Front running

For athletes who are fit and confident, front running is often the tactic of choice. For these athletes, the strategy is a simple one: You run as fast as you can for as long as you can and hopefully, the finishing line will arrive before you are spent. This may be effective against athletes of lesser ability, but eventually the runner will come up against somebody whose fitness is equal to their own. Runners with only one tactic—front running — at their disposal are easy to beat: you know exactly what they are going to do and their rivals will plan ways to beat them. The athlete that constantly changes their strategy is very difficult to beat, you don't what they are going to do next!

Front running requires the athlete to exercise good pace judgment, self discipline — i.e. not to panic if the race unfolds in a different way than they expect, and a large degree of mental concentration. Unfortunately, these qualities are not the defining traits of young children!

Common mistakes made by front running athletes

- *Starting too fast*— trying to run away from your rivals and expecting that a comfortable (and winning) lead should be established early into the race is a very common mistake committed by young athletes. Practise a fast start to establish a position and then have your athlete learn to reduce their pace to something more sustainable

- *Self discipline* — Young children tend to be reactive in a race. When a runner passes them, many feel that they immediately have to respond
- and fight off the challenge by sprinting hard to maintain the lead. This is a very draining response and is one that an experienced distance runner would avoid. Have you ever noticed that a child may break into a furious sprint when they pass in-front of mum, dad, or teacher; a few metres later they revert back to a jog. Training the children with the Fartlek and Paarluff methods will help to teach them the benefits of good pacing. The improved self discipline will come with maturation.

Getting Started in Track and Field Athletics

- A front runner has a problem if they face an equally devoted front runner. Sometimes these runners race at such a speed that both of them succeed in tiring each other out. There have been many occasions where a steady pace athlete creeps up and passes our fatigued frontrunners and claims victory. The front running athlete needs to understand that their tactic must be flexible—it is not always possible to run away from another front runner—and so the plan must be changed mid race.

- *Looking back* — Front running young athletes will often lapse into the habit of looking back (on a regular basis) to see if their rivals are catching up. Turning your head leads to very inefficient technique and your athletes should be reminded to always look forward.

- Young athletes who front run may sometimes concentrate more on their rivals than concentrating on their own running form. Train your students to silently ask themselves questions about their running technique as they run, e.g. *"is this a pace that I can keep up?" "Am I relaxed?" "When I am going to start my sprint finish?"*, etc. In this way, the children can develop their powers of concentration and, hopefully, improve the quality of their performance.

The Sitting and Kicking Tactic

The tactic that is known as "sitting and kicking" is easy to adopt but requires a firm belief in the athlete that they can out sprint their rivals in the race for the finishing line. The "sitting" aspect of this tactic refers to the way an athlete closely follows the pace of the leader (or a rival); they respond to every move, every surge or acceleration that the leading athlete makes, but they do not attempt to take the lead. Only when the finishing line is in sight does the "sitter" unleash their sprint finish.

Common mistakes made by athletes using the "sitting and kicking tactic

When the athlete adopts this tactic, they are stating by their action that they can outrun their rival in the dash to the finish. Of course, some athletes are much faster sprinters than others. Perhaps the most common mistake made by athletes whom use this technique is that they under-estimate the speed of their rivals.

Getting Started in Track and Field Athletics

When an athlete devises their race strategy, they need to try to evaluate the finishing speed of their rivals. If you know you have much better speed, sitting and kicking could be a good tactic for you. If you know that you have poor sprinting speed, you must develop another way to beat your rivals

There are occasions when an athlete becomes so focused on following their rivals that they leave their sprint finish far too late. The timing of a sprint finish is critical. If you start it too soon you may struggle in the last few metres, leave it too late and you deny yourself the chance for success. Have a plan—a decision as to when you will sprint and the belief that you can sustain this to the finish.

Surging

This distance running tactic can have a devastating effect on your rivals. When the running pace seems constant, all of a sudden an athlete may decide to "*surge*" - this means they accelerate and start running at a much faster pace for a distance that only they know. The other athletes in the race are then faced with troubling questions: Can this surging athlete maintain this pace until the finish? If I decide not to match this speed, will I let my rival build a lead that I cannot catch? Surging requires a high level of fitness and the ability to change pace without it robbing you of your chance to finish the race well. This tactic is particularly effective for an athlete whom has poor sprinting speed. Rather than leaving your final effort to the end of the race—and running the risk of being defeated by a fast sprinter—these athletes are encourage to practice surging. The surging tactic—if delivered at unpredictable times in the race—is a good way to take the "sting" out of the sprint finishers.

Common mistakes made with surging

This tactic is only effective if the athlete conserves enough energy to complete the race. Some young athletes may surge so hard that their subsequent pace falls off to a slow jog. The idea is to be able to alternate between fast, faster, and medium paces.

Good mental discipline is needed with this tactic. If the athlete maintains the surge for too long, again, they might only succeed in ruining their chances. A surge is a temporary increase in pace, not a permanent one. Athletes who cannot control their impulse to surge and then keep running faster and faster are doomed to early fatigue!

Getting Started in Track and Field Athletics

A close and exciting race nears its end!

Getting Started in Track and Field Athletics

Working your way through

In this tactic, the runner starts off at a slower pace compared to the rest of the field. It is not unusual for an athlete using this strategy to find them significantly behind the leader. As the pace of the fast starting athletes slow, our steady starting athlete now moves by one athlete after another. This tactic can give the athlete confidence as they steadily improve their position. This is a good strategy to use for the athlete that is not blessed with good speed. Relying on their strength to sustain a strong pace throughout the race will help this athlete to be more successful than trying to keep up with the faster starting athletes. The most common mistake is when athletes allow the leaders to establish such a large lead that they cannot close the gap before the finishing line. An athlete using this strategy must stay close enough to the leader to allow this tactic to work.

Teachers Corner

As with so many track and field events, relaxation and efficiency of movement are significant contributors to sporting success. Errors in distance running—such as over striding— are easy to observe; long loping strides devoid of power, jarring movements. Having your athletes correct problems with stride patterns is best dealt with through an experiential running. Have your athletes run 400m at 50 % of their distance running race pace. It is likely that this athlete will not over-stride and will run with a relaxed gait. Have the athlete concentrate on the feel of this pace, think about the stride, this is easy running. After complete rest, have this athlete run 400m fast but trying to run with the same feel as the first run. With practice, the athlete will eventually learn to run relaxed at speed.

Getting Started in Track and Field Athletics

Creating your tactical plan

Many athletes will go into a running race and "just run." However, with a small amount of preparation—discussion with coaches, teachers, parents—each athlete is capable of running so much better. Previous experience is always valuable as long as you can learn from the successes and setbacks of that race. Ask yourself *"what went well, and what could I do better?"* Honest answers to those two questions are a good starting point in developing a race plan. Flexibility in the tactical plan is essential. Remember: you are not the only runner in the race with a tactical plan. Sometimes an athlete does something that is unpredictable and forces you to change your plan in the middle of the race.

- Consider your strengths—what do you do well? Are you an excellent sprinter? Can you run at the front with confidence, or do you need to apply the surging tactic to help you succeed?

- What are your weaknesses? Do you allow yourself to drop the pace in the middle of the race? Do you allow your rivals to dictate the race and do you always feel that you are responding?

- What are the strengths and weaknesses of your rivals? Do you see them using the same tactics every single race? How can you use this knowledge to beat them next time?

- Emphasize effort not outcome. You cannot control the pace or tactics of anyone else other than your self. If someone comes along and runs so much faster than you do not view this as a setback or failure. If you have truly given your best effort, than you should take pride in your performance.

Getting Started in Track and Field Athletics

Fartlek Running

This is a Swedish word that apparently translates as "speed play" (it also happens to be a word that induces giggles and comparisons to other bodily noises with your students!) Fartlek is a method of training that is very effective in developing speed, endurance and improving your athletes general fitness levels. The concept is a fairly simple one: running on trails or around fields, the runner will start off with a few minutes of gentle jogging. Once warmed up, they may decide to sprint from one tree to the next (perhaps a distance of 50m). The amount of rest is determined by the athlete. When ready, the athlete runs fast again – a different distance and perhaps at a different speed. The key to Fartlek running is to have the athlete run a variety of distances and speeds and also take different amounts of rest (i.e. total rest, walking and jogging rest, or perhaps fast jogging rest.)

This type of running is very unstructured – i.e. it is up to the athlete to decide when to run and for how long. The emphasis should be on speed that the athlete can hold comfortably for a sustained period.

Fartlek training is particularly useful for athletes who are in need of a change of scenery – away from the track. This method of distance running training is effective if used as an aerobic training technique. If the young athlete takes insufficient rest, they may become anaerobic and (as discussed in other sections of this book) unable to complete the workout.

Key points to remember

Emphasise relaxed technique, good speed, and sustained running. Do not run so fast that you need a very long rest – this is aerobic training and you are exercising your heart and lungs and training your body to efficiently carry oxygen to the muscles.

Getting Started in Track and Field Athletics

How long should my athletes use fartlek training?

After a warm-up, have your athletes run the following:

Grade 2 students — 3/ 5 minutes of running. Include runs of 50m, 100m, 200m, and 400m.

Grade 3 students — 5 minutes of running. Include runs of 50m, 100m, 200m, and 400m

Grade 4 students — 5 – 7 minutes of running. Include runs of 50m, 100m, 200m, and 400m

Grade 5 students 7 – 8 minutes of running. Include runs of 100m, 200m, and one run of 600m

Grade 6 students 8 – 10 minutes of running. Include runs of 100m, 200, and 1 run of 800m

Grade 7 students 8 – 12 minutes of running. Include runs of 50m, 200m, and several runs between 600m and 800m.

Teachers Corner

Fartlek running will be an attractive training technique for young children who may find running difficult. Drawing on the principles of a differentiated classroom, this method of training allows the teacher to challenge the competent athlete and make the workout appealing to the less athletic. As the resting period is up to each individual athlete, the un-athletic child may feel more at ease with the demands of this session over a structured workout (set distances and set rests). The only cautionary note for teachers and coaches to be aware of is that some athletes may not push themselves too hard and then take too much rest; you will have to monitor this.

Getting Started in Track and Field Athletics
Paarluff Running

Paarluff is a word from Finland that describes endurance running working with a partner. This is a very good activity for children of all ranges of ability. The athlete is paired with another—sometimes of the same ability, sometimes you might decide to have runners paired with vastly different abilities. The race is held around a track for an exact number of minutes e.g. 3—5 minutes according to their age. Unlike a relay race that has the runners completing pre– defined distances, a Paarluff race has the athletes running different distances; distances that they decide that they want to run. Before the race starts, each pair discuss their strategy for the race. Perhaps the first runner will sprint to establish a lead, then the second runner runs several laps of the track while the first runner is recovering. Another pair might decide that they will run even distances e.g. 200m each. Another team might decide to alternate between sprinting and distance running (e.g *"you run 100m, I will run 800m, you then run 800m and I will run 100m,"etc*). The key point is that there are no rules that tell you how much or how little you have to run. Athletes may need to jog across the inside field of the track in order to takeover from their partner—that is okay in Paarluff running. The team that is in the lead at the end of the 5 minutes (or however long you decide the race should be for your athletes), wins the race.

> Paarluff races can be very exciting as the lead often changes hands many times.

Whatever tactic each pair uses, this is an activity that is very useful in teaching children to avoid some of the most common mistakes in distance running: Pace judgement is a critical skill in distance running. Some groups will start way too fast and will eventually be beaten by a team that has run a more even pace. Relaxed running with good technique is essential if the athlete is to either avoid early fatiguing, or cope with it at the latter stages of the race.

Getting Started in Track and Field Athletics

How long should my athletes do Paarluff Racing?

This type of racing—for children of this age — is meant to be a fun form of aerobic training. If the children sprint and take very little recovery, they will rapidly exhaust themselves as the poorly conditioned anaerobic energy system kicks in. The coach / teacher will need to emphasize that self control and good pace judgement is needed if they are to carry this exercise out correctly. For their first attempt, have them run for 2—3 minutes. Many— if not all—will race too fast too soon and struggle. Use this first run as a reference point *"you see what happens when you don't pace yourself?"* Once they have learned how to run the race I recommend the following race periods:

Grade 2 students— 3 minutes
Grade 3 students— 3 minutes
Grade 4 students— 3—6 minutes
Grade 5 students— 4—6 minutes
Grade 6 students— 5—7 minutes
Grade 7 students—5—7 minutes

This can be either a very intense workout for the children or a gentle one that works on running at rhythm and with good technique. The coaches instructional preamble will help the athletes know what is expected from the workout and how best to achieve its goal.

Getting Started in Track and Field Athletics

Four corners running

This is an easy activity for your athletes to work on their technique, develop a sense of pace judgment, and work on their aerobic fitness. Split your class into 4 equal size groups (mix the abilities and genders) and send one group to each of the four corners of a very large square you have marked out on a field. You could make the square 100m by 100m, or even 200m by 200m of you so wish. Tell your athletes that they will be running for 3/ 4/ 5 minutes (match to the age group) and that this is a distance workout. Some athletes will make the mistake of treating this as a sprint and will quickly tire.

The athletes of the first group (A) will run from their corner to the next (as if they were about to run around a square). When the first runner arrives at that cone, the group waiting at that cone (B) runs to next corner, the process is repeated for the next group. Group C will run to group D. Group D then has to run 2 straights (because there is no group waiting for them at the corner in front of them as that was where group A started). The process repeats for 3 /4 / 5 minutes—whatever you set.

This activity is very good for un-athletic children as they can be anonymous in the group—no-one is watching them bring along the rear as would be the case with interval running.

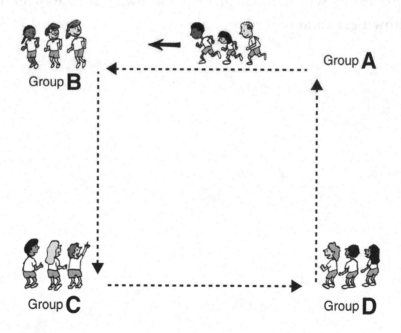

Getting Started in Track and Field Athletics
Huddle Ball

Having children do a traditional distance workout—e.g. intervals with jogging recovery— may be attractive to your capable athletes. However, for the un-athletic these workouts tend to expose difficulties with endurance and may not be enjoyable activities. One game that can challenge the athletic and yet allow slower athletes to work at their own level is the game Huddle ball.

Split your group into two equal sized teams. You can play with any number of athletes, preferably, the more the better. One team stands at the end of a field—perhaps 50—80m away, and will have to "defend" their team's end. The attacking team gather into a huddle and decide which athlete will carry a tennis ball. All the athletes on the attacking team then pretend to carry the ball by cupping their hands and holding them close to their stomachs. When the attacking team breaks from the huddle, their task is to run to the defending team's end and cross a line without being tagged by the defenders. If they succeed, they score 1 point for their team. If the person carrying the tennis ball crosses the line without being tagged, 10 points are scored. If tagged you just stand still and wait till all athletes either cross the line or are caught (this only takes a few seconds so nobody is inactive for long). Once the points are tallied, the attacking team jogs quickly back to their end and now prepare to become defenders. The process is repeated for as many "ends" as you decide.

The beauty of this game is that athletes who will cringe at the prospect of 20—30 minutes of sustained running, will forget time as they get involved in this game. Huddle ball blends sprinting (as each athlete either tries to out run or catch and opponent) and endurance running.

There are few rules in Huddle ball. The only caution is that some athletes may walk or jog very slowly each time it is their turn to attack. Encouraging these athletes to bring some speed and energy to the task may be needed.

Getting Started in Track and Field Athletics

Capture the Flag

This game, popular in many schools, has a number of different rules. When played with the purpose of achieving a distance running workout, it can be a good way to have children of different levels of fitness work hard. The beauty of this game is that un-athletic children get lost in the flow of the game and can work at their own rate without feeling humiliated for being at the back of a run. If the coach can encourage the children to sprint hard, and keep jogging during "rest" periods, the physiological training benefits will be significant. The coach must ensure that the athletes bring an appropriate effort to this game, it is easy for some kids to become lazy in this game and the coach may have monitor this. The rules are many in this game but I will try to present a simplified version here:

- Split your class into two groups.
- At each end of the field is a large square (5m x 5m) in which 4 relay batons are placed.
- The object of the game is for one team to steal the other team's relay batons. If all relay batons are in one square, the game is won and then can be re-started.
- The game is played for a certain length of time 20 – 30 minutes is recommended.
- The field is divided into two by a line of cones.
- Each team is safe when they are in their own half.
- If they are tagged in the other team's half, they must go to a prison / holding area which is located in the other team's half.
- Tagged athletes can be set free by a teammate running over to the prison and tagging your hand.
- If athletes have been in the prison for too long the coach should shout "jail break" and all athletes may run out of the jail.

Getting Started in Track and Field Athletics

Devil takes the hindmost

This is an activity that is borrowed from the sport of cycling. Have your athletes run around a small track (200m per lap max). After a few laps of steady state running, inform the athletes that the Devil takes the hindmost concept is now in play. At the end of each lap, the last runner (or last 2/3/4 runners—you can decide how many) are eliminated from the race. The battle—as the race unfolds—is stay away from elimination as long as possible. The final two runners then race it out for the win.

You will need to apply some restricting rules for your better athletes otherwise they will just sprint to the front, establish a huge lead, and the race will lose its appeal. For your slower athletes, you might like to have a race just for them, or they will be the first to be eliminated and not enjoy the practice benefits of this race. Place a time limit on the race so that it stays within the recommended range for athletes of their age.

Premium racing (for house points)

This format is also borrowed from cycling. In very long cycling races, the organizers will attempt to create excitement and change race strategy by inserting a race "premium." The premium is a prize that is awarded to the athlete that is in the lead at the designated stage of the race. The premiums can be announced before the race starts or randomly announced throughout the race.

You can adapt this concept in your training programmes with young distance runners. In my classes we have a "house system" where students work to earn House points in an on-going competition throughout the school year. This recognition system can be used to reward athletes who demonstrate good form and effort. Have your runners run slowly around the track and have them work on technique. Tell them to relax their shoulders, think about their stride length, keep their heads still, etc. Then, as they are focusing on their technique, announce the first 3—5 runners across the line will get a "House point". There may be a mad sprint for the line, immediately tell the runners they must resume their jogging and concentrate on relaxing their technique.

Getting Started in Track and Field Athletics

You might like to reward house points for runners who demonstrate excellent technique while racing for the line—this will give the less athletic child a chance to win points for their team. You could also offer premium points for effort—not just being first across the line.

Elastic band running

Have your athletes run for a certain time, e.g. 45 seconds to 1 minute. Tell them that they will be repeating this run 4/5 times. The challenge is to imagine that they are an elastic band that is being stretched just that little bit further with each run. Can they run further than the previous run? This is an introduction to interval running and will help children learn the value of pacing themselves. Athletes that start too fast will not succeed in beating the distance of their previous run. The rest time between each run is dependent on the age of the runner. You do not want full recovery as this is a distance workout with an emphasis on pacing and efficiency.

Let's go the races!
(handicapping)

This can be a fun activity as long as it is presented with sensitivity and respect for slower athletes in the group. Handicapping is a concept borrowed from horse racing. In order to make a horse race more exciting, horses rated as fast may be expected to carry some lead weights in their saddles—this invariably slows them down and gives the slower horses a chance to be competitive. This concept is adapted to track running in the following way: Rank your athletes fastest to slowest. If you are racing over 100m, have your fastest runner start on the start line (or scratch as it can sometimes be called). All other athletes—who are considered to be slower are given a head start. The distance of this head start varies, the slowest may have a 20m lead over the fastest runner, while the 2nd fastest runner in your group may only have a 2/3 m lead. In theory, when the race is run, all of your runners should be very close to one another as they approach the finishing line.

The children love this race, although you must read the emotional reactions of your slower athletes as you place them along the track. If this is presented in the wrong way, some kids might feel humiliated.

Getting Started in Track and Field Athletics

Handicapping races can be run over distances as well as sprints. The challenge can be for your talented athletes to work hard and make up lots of ground in order to win. For your slower athletes, the challenge is to see if they can hold off the faster runners in the race for the finishing line.

Can we beat the World Record?

An activity that my students love to play is where you chose a race—perhaps the 1500m and have each runner race a small section in relay format. The target is to see how close to the World record for men and women the team has run. This activity helps to put the record into a perspective that the children understand.

Esti-Win

This is a simple activity for your endurance runs. Have the children do a fitness run (a time trial) that requires them to give their best effort. Record their times. A few days later repeat the run but ask the children to predict their finishing time. Tell them their times from the previous run. The student closest to their predicted time wins the race. This allows athletes who are at the back to be competitive.

Getting Started in Track and Field Athletics
Sample distance running workouts
Grade 2

30 minute class
Maximum recommended distance: 800m

Warm – up
Play games of tag to get the children warm. There are many themes: Tails, team tails, stuck in the mud, etc.

Do a few minutes of stretching where you work on the major muscle groups. Have an influential student lead the exercises.

Do 4-6 strides—these are fast runs over 30—50m. Concentrate on good technique and relaxation. Make sure the students run fast and don't just go through the motions.

Skill / fitness building
3 minutes of 4 corners running— Many of the children will make the mistake of running too fast in the first minute and will slow significantly. Give them complete rest and then repeat.

Finish with some running games
Mark out a small square. Have 1 chaser. If you are caught put on a pinny and become a chaser as well. The object is to stay "alive" for as long as you can. If you run outside the square you are caught. Other games are suggested in the distance running games inventory.

Getting Started in Track and Field Athletics
Grade 3

30 minute lesson
Maximum recommended distance (in either practise or racing) 1km

Warm up
Jog 400m and then go straight into some games (refer to the games inventory)
4-6 fast strides over 50m – run with a friend. Emphasize speed.

Skill building / fitness development
3-4 minute Paarluff, or
3 minutes of four corner running or
800m – pacing run
15 minutes of Capture the Flag

Games to finish
Refer to the games inventory and play a number of tag games to finish.

Getting Started in Track and Field Athletics
Grades 4 / 5

30 minute workout
Maximum recommended distance 1 – 1.5km

Warm-up
600m run
Stretching routine 4-6 minutes
4-6 strides from 40 – 60 metres working on acceleration, running at speed with relaxation

or

10 minutes of Capture the Flag (ensure that the children are running at all times)

or

6 minutes of different tag games.

Stretching and Strides

Skill Building / Fitness development
1km pacing run – run the first 500m relaxed then accelerate steadily over the next 500m.

Another way to run this 1km run is to practise surging – structured i.e. on the coaches whistle for about 100m, or unstructured i.e. for varying distances whenever the athlete feels able. Each lesson may provide the opportunity to learn how to apply some of the tactics as discussed in earlier pages.

3-6 minutes of Fartlek or Paarluff running.

6 fast runs over 60m slightly faster than distance running speed with the athlete concentrating on relaxation and other aspects of technique (head still, good arm carriage, etc).

Games to finish

Getting Started in Track and Field Athletics
Grades 6/7

40 minute class
Maximum recommended distance 2 – 2.5km

Some of your students may find running for these distances very challenging. Design your class around the abilities of your students. For those that are capable, have them run at pace over extended distances; e.g. a workout such as 4-6 x 500m with 3 minutes rest will be possible. A distance running ladder 1minute –2 – 3 – 2- 1minute runs with the rest time the same as the run – will be a good distance workout for your capable athlete. The athlete will make a mess of this session if they sprint – become anaerobic – and not complete the workout. The emphasis will be on running at pace with control and self-discipline. Such workouts will be difficult for some athletes. Have them play Capture the Flag, Huddle Ball, partner Paarluff for 4-6 minutes as alternatives.

Steady state running over 2km with the athlete injecting surges, accelerations, etc is another way to practise skills and develop fitness. As with the sample workouts with the other grades, stretching, strides, and fun games should augment the body of the workout.

The Jumping Events

Getting Started in Track and Field Athletics

The History of Long Jumping

Like many of the activities that formed the basis of the ancient Olympic Games, long jumping was used to test the fighting skills of the Greek warriors. Soldiers heading into battle were expected to have, not only excellent skill in wrestling and throwing javelins, but they were also expected to be able to jump across fast flowing rivers. Long jumpers at these ancient games used hand-held objects called Halteres (see picture below) to help them reach great distances.

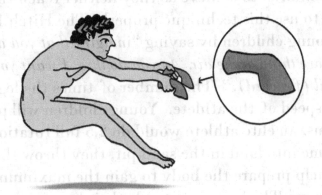

It is no coincidence that some of the World's greatest long jumpers have also been some of the greatest sprinters. William de Hart Hubbard—the man considered to have been the creator of the "Hitch Kick" technique (to be covered later) was also the world record holder for the 100 yards. The great Jesse Owens was the Olympic Champion for sprinting and long jumping, a feat copied by American Carl Lewis. The German athlete Heike Dreschler was also Olympic sprint and long jumping champion. Marion Jones, Sydney Olympic Games 100m Champion also finished 3rd in the long jump. The pattern is clear: **Speed on the runway is critical if you want to jump a long way.**

Long jump World Records

The world record for the men's long jump is 8m.95cms set by Mike Powell of the USA in 1991.

The world record for the women's long jump is 7m.52cms set by Galina Chistykova from Russia set in 1988.

Getting Started in Track and Field Athletics

Techniques of Long Jump

There are, essentially, two techniques:

- The Hitch Kick
- The Hang technique

The **Hitch Kick** is a complicated skill that is used to counter balance the body's tendency to rotate as it moves through the air. The Hitch Kick is difficult for young children to achieve as they neither reach the speed nor height in the jump to use this technique properly. The Hitch Kick can be best described to young children by saying *"imagine that you are cycling on an air bicycle as you move through the air. As you do this, I want you to swing your arms like a windmill (forward)."* The number of times the legs will "cycle" will depend on the speed of the athlete. Young children will probably only manage 1.5 rotations, an elite athlete would do 2.5 full rotations. As the athlete starts to come into land in the sand pit, they throw their arms forward, this will help prepare the body to gain the maximum amount of distance from the jump. The jumper extends their legs forward—this is known as the leg shoot. The jump is only considered to be over when the athlete has left the sand pit.

Getting Started in Track and Field Athletics

The Hang technique

This technique is much easier for young children to master. With a fast run-up and then takeoff, the jumper throws their arms up into the air and "hangs." The picture below demonstrates the technique much easier than words. As the athlete comes into land their legs extend forward (the leg shoot) in the same way as with the hitch kick technique.

The rules of long jumping

The athlete is permitted to take 3 jumps. At a major championship, the top six athletes will also be granted an additional three jumps. The winner of the competition is the athlete that jumps the furthest and has observed all of the rules.

The athlete is allowed to take a maximum of 2 minutes per jump. If they take any longer, the jump is over and they have no distance recorded.

The athlete is not obliged to take each jump. The judges will call the name of each athlete in order and the athlete can call out "pass" if they don't want to take a jump. If you decline, you may not take that particular jump at a later date. So why would you pass up the opportunity to jump? Sometimes, an athlete may decide to rest in order to preserve their energy for a big jump.

Getting Started in Track and Field Athletics

The athlete must take off either on, or before the take-off board. If the jump is acceptable (with respect to this rule) the judge will raise a white flag – this indicates to the spectators that the jump was valid. An illegal jump is indicated by the judge raising a red flag.

On the take off board there is a small strip of plasticene. Any imprint that is made on this strip informs the judge that the jump is illegal.

For a record jump to count, the jump must be completed with a following wind of less that 2m/second.

The athlete must take off with one foot. Two footed jumps are illegal.

The technique used must be not be dangerous to the athlete or any other person. This may seem a strange rule but it was incorporated to prevent somersaults through the air (as was experimented with in the 1970's).

When the athlete lands in the long jump pit, the jump is only considered to be over when the athlete has left the pit. The athlete must also walk out the front of the pit. The jump is measured from the takeoff board to the last mark that they made in the sand that is closest to the takeoff board – this means that if they fall back into the pit and extend a hand the measurement is taken to the hand not where the athlete landed.

Getting Started in Track and Field Athletics

Common mistakes made in long jumping

- *Some young athletes fail to actually jump.* They run at the pit and basically "step" into it. This may be a confidence issue and something that could be rectified with practise.

- *Taking off before or after the board.* A world class long jumper knows how many paces they will need to take in their approach to the take-off board. The key variant in hitting the board is the speed in the athlete's approach. If they change their speed each time they jump, it is difficult for them to consistently hit the board. Again, practise and experience— learning from mistakes—will help the athlete understand how to hit the takeoff board without looking for it.

- *Too long a run-up*— Young children will often believe that the longer the run up, the better they will jump. Some of these run-ups are so long that they athlete is slowing down considerably by the time they reach the take-off board. Remind the children that they need to be at their top speed when they hit the board. I suggest a run-up of 20—25m is sufficient.

- *Walking out the back of the pit (i.e. close to the takeoff board).* This results in the jump being recorded at the last mark that the athlete makes closest to the board. Remind the children of the rule that states how the jump is measured.

- *The athlete fails to use the "leg shoot" technique.* For the athletes to reach the full benefits of the jump they extend their legs as they come into land, in this way they can add considerable distance to the jump. Teaching the children the principles behind leg shoot and demonstrating with an athlete whom uses this technique will help these athletes learn this technique.

Getting Started in Track and Field Athletics

Long Jump Games

12 steps to take-off!

This game is designed to test how close the athlete can get to the takeoff board without stepping over it. Each athlete is allowed only 12 steps in their approach run (no more, no less). The athlete runs in—counting their 12 steps—and then jumps. The distance of the jump is not important in this game, just the distance from where the athlete took off and the board. The object of this exercise is to have the athletes practise running and jumping without having to look for, or anticipate by slowing down, the take-off board. Also the athlete will learn that their speed must be consistent every time they run if they are to hit the take-off board accurately. If their speed varies with these 12 strides, they will need to adjust their starting point.

Further and further

In this activity the athlete is asked to jump at 50% effort. Ask the athlete to concentrate on relaxation, not looking for the take-off board, use a leg shoot on landing. Draw a line across the sandpit where the athlete lands. Repeat this exercise only this time ask the athlete to increase their effort—not to their best—but 75%. Ask the athlete to jump across the line drawn in the sand but with relaxation of effort emphasised. Another line is drawn. The process is repeated for the 3rd time with a maximum effort now required. Remind the athlete of all the important technical points—especially relaxation.

Guess your distance

If you watch the world's best jumpers, they often know when a jump has been good and when it is sub-standard. This comes with years of practice. A fun activity is to have your athletes guess how far they have jumped. Measure accurately with the tape measure and inform the athlete after they have guessed. On their next few jumps it will be interesting to see if they become better at guessing.

Getting Started in Track and Field Athletics

And the winner is ....

One of the goals of this book is to teach children to appreciate the skills and performances of others (whether it be their friends or the performances of the world's greatest athletes). This activity gives the children the opportunity to apply their knowledge of the skill—in this case long jump—in a fun way. Itemize all the things you would like to see athlete do in their jump, example: Have your athletes judge the performance of the jumper on these criteria and give a score out of 10.

(1)   The athlete has a run-up that is not too long or too short
(2)   The athlete approaches the jump with good speed
(3)   The athlete does not slow down in anticipation of the board
(4)   The athlete hits the take-off board
(5)   The athlete gets good height at takeoff
(6)   The athlete employs the hitch kick or hang technique
(7)   The athlete throws their arms forward to increase distance
(8)   The athlete uses the leg shoot on landing
(9)   The athlete doesn't put their hand back on landing
(10) The athlete walks out the front of the pit

What is important is not so much the score, but the fact that the children assessing their friend, and the athlete competing are learning how to analyse and apply the skills they have been taught. Tell the athlete which areas you feel that they need to improve. You can use video tape to help reinforce the athlete's understanding of their successes and weaknesses in this area.

Getting Started in Track and Field Athletics

Standing long jump and long jump off 3 strides

Standing long jump was an event that was part of the ancient Greek Olympics Games. The athletes would hold hand weights called Halteres and use them to gain extra distance in their jump. The athlete would swing their arms around in a windmill motion then hurl themselves forward. Using Halteres may not be possible but have your athletes compete with one another. This event could be used in the gym (a rainy day activity) and unlike outdoor long jump, you can have lots of jumpers competing at the same time. An extension of this activity is to have your athletes jump for distance but with only a three stride approach run. The emphasis would be on getting a good take-off—placing the foot firmly on the board and getting lots of vertical lift. This activity could also be applied in the gym.

Jump to it!
Teaching long jump in a gym

Bad weather sometimes limits the availability of the long jump pit, however that is no reason for you to completely suspend the teaching of this event. You can use a gymnastics springboard to assist in the teaching of the hang and hitch kick techniques. Have your athletes run up to the spring board and get lots of height (remind them to take off with one foot not two feet which is the norm in gymnastics when using this piece of equipment). The extra height gained gives the athlete time to utilize the two techniques much more efficiently. A soft landing is essential and I suggest that you bring out the high jump mat to help you. This is a fun way to practice long jump for children.

Jump for points!

Split your class into two teams that are evenly matched in talent. Mark out zones in the long jump (by drawing lines across the pit). Award a point for each zone (1point for the zone closest to the take-off board, 2,3,4,5 points for the zone furthest from the take-off board. Each zone could be 1m—that is up to you to decide). The athlete earns the points for their team according to the zone that they land in. Keep track of the totals.

Speed Jumping is a variant of this activity. Have your athletes form two teams then complete as many jumps as they can in 1 minute. Keep count of points. Safety rule: No athlete can start to jump until the previous athlete has left the pit .

Getting Started in Track and Field Athletics

High Jump

Numerous techniques have been used over the years for high jump. As the heights cleared by the athletes have reached ever higher, some of these techniques can no longer be used as the soft foam landing mats were not used. In the past, athletes would jump into sand pits or saw-dust mounds! No event in track and field has been so creative in naming various techniques:

- The Western Roll
- The Straddle
- The Scissors
- The Brill Bend
- The Fosbury Flop

The Western roll technique required the athlete to take a fast approach to the high jump bar starting from the side. Taking off with one foot (as is the rule for all high jump techniques) the athlete would literally roll / or spin their body up, and over the bar. This technique was refined and became known as the

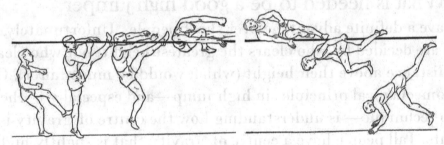

Straddle technique. For many years, the Straddle technique was used by the world's best athletes. This skill requires the athlete to take off with the foot that is closest to the takeoff bar—then swing their other leg upward. As the body reaches it's highest point the athlete then 'rolls" over the bar. Very few athletes today use either of these techniques.

Getting Started in Track and Field Athletics

The same can be said for the **Scissors technique,** this technique might be popular with children but the principles of biomechanics that determine how well an athlete might jump (using the centre of gravity to your \advantage, transferring speed and momentum into height, utilizing the mechanical principles of levers, etc) are not effectively applied with this technique—thus it is not used by serious athletes.

What is needed to be a good high jumper?

Tall people have a definite advantage over short people. Unfortunately, the competitions are decided by who clears the greatest height, not who clears the greatest distance above their height (which would be much fairer). One of the key biomechanical principles in high jump—and especially in the Fosbury Flop technique— is understanding how the centre of gravity is used to clear heights. Tall people have a centre of gravity that is slightly higher (when clearing the high jump bar) and this places them at an advantage over short people.

Getting Started in Track and Field Athletics

The Fosbury Flop

The technique most frequently used by serious athletes is the Fosbury Flop; this was named after American athlete Dick Fosbury whom experimented with this technique in the late 1960's. The Brill Bend—named after Canadian athlete Debbie Brill—also employed the same biomechanical principles.

Many children will experiment with techniques that revolve around the theme of diving head first over the bar, something we have named "The Superman" technique. If the athlete takes off on one foot the jump would be legal but limited in its potential for reaching height. Coaches who only have one high jump mat may want to note that their is considerable risk for children whom dive forward to fall off the end of the mat. Remind your children the jump is for height not length! Impress on your athletes that learning and applying new techniques (i.e. the Fosbury Flop) will allow them to jump much higher. Sports scientists have repeatedly shown that athletes who train with the Flop technique have better results and improve faster.

- Approach to the bar
- Take-off
- Flight over the bar
- Landing

The approach run

Speed is an important part of the approach run but is only useful if it can be controlled and effectively used by the athlete. Charging at the bar at full speed and not being able to apply the principles of the Flop technique will not help the athlete clear the bar. Some the world's great jumpers are so well trained that they can "attack" (sprint) the bar with great speed and utilize this energy. Other athletes start slow in their approach run and then sprint the last few strides. The key is the very last step which transfers all this horizontal energy into vertical lift.

Getting Started in Track and Field Athletics

The approach run with the Fosbury Flop is a curved run (like an inverted "J" shape). A typical approach would be 9 strides. In the first 6 strides the athlete will approach the bar straight, the final strides the athlete curves towards the bar and prepares their body for take-off.

Mistakes that children make in the approach run

- Running straight at the bar
- Leaving their curve too late
- Running too fast / too slow
- Not using their arms to prepare themselves for take-off
- Slowing down as they approach the bar
- Taking lots of little "stutter steps" in their approach

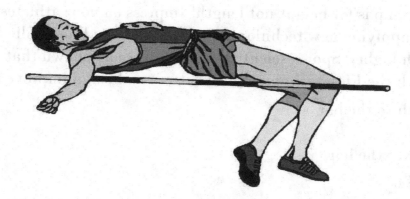

Man versus animal — a high jump competition

In the animal kingdom, mankind is not a particularly impressive creature when it comes to athletic feats. We are out-sprinted by Cheetahs. We are relative weaklings compared to the beetle that can lift a weight the equivalent of an army tank easily above its head. In high jumping the competition is not even close. The world record for men currently stands at 2m 47. The best performance by an animal (I can't imagine who scientifically gathered this data!) is apparently the mighty Flea. For a human to match the high jumping skills of a flea, we would have to jump over the Eiffel Tower!

Getting Started in Track and Field Athletics

Take-off

The aim of the take-off is to transfer the speed from the approach into vertical lift. To do this the last step (stride) acts as a brake. The foot slams down and the knee bends, as the leg springs and straightens out lift is generated. Try to jump with out bending your knees—it's practically impossible. The knee bend is necessary to help with the transfer of the speed. Biomechanic analysts have stated that the approach speed is reduced by about 50%. The take-off leg for Fosbury Flop is different to that of the Straddle. Standing sideways to the bar, the take off leg for the Flop is the one that is furthest away from the bar. The closest leg swings upward with the assistance of the arms that have been pulled back at the last second and then swung forward to help generate lift. The outside leg (or plant, as it is sometimes called) turns then lifts. The incredible forces that move through the take-off leg have been known to cause strain to ligaments in that ankle (severe pronation). Any of your athletes with week ankles should be cautious.

Mistakes that children make in the "take-off phase"

- Some children will take-off too far away from the bar (and run the risk of landing on the floor. As a safety precaution, place some masking tape on the gym floor / sports field and insist that your athletes take-off after the taped line. Taking off too close to the bar prevents the athlete from getting into the flop position and utilizing the benefits of their approach.

- Taking off too close to the high jump stands. With the curved approach, some young athletes will have considerable momentum that carries them up and forward (rather than mostly upward as is the case for experienced jumpers). This presents a serious risk for such a child for as they move through the air they may either hit the high jump stand (that balances the bar) or miss the soft landing mat completely. Instruct your athletes to takeoff no later than the mid-point of the bar no matter which side they are running from.

- Taking off with the wrong leg. It is impossible to execute the Flop taking off with the leg closest to bar. Athletes attempting this may find themselves tangled up and crashing into the bar without much of a jump.

Getting Started in Track and Field Athletics

Flight

Every segment of movement through the air has been analysed by biomechanic experts looking for efficiency in the use of centre of gravity, and body rotation. This is very advanced technical training and is well beyond the scope of this book (and the ability of young children to use this in formation). What follows is a basic summary of the Flop technique in the flight phase. After take-off, the body moves upward and then—with the athlete's arching of their back—reaches the peak of their jump. A good jump will see the highest point of the arc, and the centre of gravity, being reached over the bar. Athletes that take off too soon or too late will find that the peak of their jump is reached before or after the bar—usually with the result that the jump fails. Note the difference in the two pictures, the first athlete is "sitting down" and has a low (if non existent arch over the bar). This athlete is unlikely to reach great heights unless he learns to arch his back.

The athlete pictured below has a much better Flop position over the bar. With hips raised high, and the back arched, the centre of gravity is at its highest point and the athlete can clearly attempt even greater heights.

Getting Started in Track and Field Athletics

The Landing Phase

As the athlete arches their back over the bar, they must now concentrate on flicking their legs upward. The legs—naturally—trail the rest of the body in using the Flop technique. There have been many examples where an athlete has cleared record breaking heights with their body only to knock the bar off with trailing legs. Several rules of high jumping must also be recognized; the jump is not considered to be over until the athlete has climbed off the landing mat. This is an important rule to remember. Sometimes an athlete may hit the bar and when the athlete has landed, the bar may still be rattling on the stands. If the bar falls off after the athlete has left the mat, the jump is valid. If the bar falls off while the athlete is on the mat...the jump is counted as a failure.

The Teachers Corner
Women normally exceed their body height by a maximum of 25 cm, men by about 50 cm (the American Franklin Jacobs was 1.73 m tall and jumped 2.32 m, i.e. a difference of 59 cm).

The high jump bar versus the rope

Should a teacher use a high jump pole, an elastic, or a rope to create the bar in high jump practices / competitions? Each has its advantages and problems. The accepted bar at official competitions is made of fibre glass. It bends but can hurt a young athlete's back if they land directly upon it. While it may offer authenticity in the practice, I would advise you to use a thin rope or long elastic. If you choose a thin rope, **do not** tie it to the high jump stands. Tying to the upright will pull the metal stand over (and possibly onto the jumper). Have two coaches manually hold the rope. If the jumper fails to make the height, you let the rope drop. One of the benefits of using the rope / elastic is that you can allow it to go slack for a jumper whom you know will struggle to achieve a reasonable height.

Getting Started in Track and Field Athletics

The rules of high jumping

The rules of this event are relatively simple but the means by which the winner is determined can be very complicated. First, the rules:

- An athlete is allowed 3 jumps at each height. The athlete may elect to pass a height (not take any jumps). Thus, it is possible for an athlete to win a competition with only one jump—assuming that everybody else has failed the height that our athlete is attempting to clear.

- The athlete must take off with one foot.

- If the athlete breaks the plane of the bar the jump is said to have taken place. This means that if an athlete is running up to the bar and at the last moment believes that their approach is wrong, they are allowed to stop and re-start their run. However, if they have placed a foot, or arm, etc, under the bar, the jump has been taken and they are judged to have failed.

- The athlete has 2 minutes to prepare and take the jump. As indicated above, the athlete may stop in the approach phase and start again. However, they do not get another 2 minutes, the jump must be taken in the remaining time.

Chair Jumping

One activity you might like to try with your high jumpers is what we call "Chair Jumping" Place a chair with the chair back right next to the landing mat. Your athlete will stand on the chair with the their back to the mat. When ready they have to jump onto the mat by arching their back and flicking their feet upward. This action mimics the position of the Fosbury flop. Depending on the length of the mat, you can have two chairs to speed up the waiting time for each student.

Once the jumpers have a feel for this activity, you could add the high jump bar or rope so that they have to arch their backs to complete a succesful jump. Safety note: Make sure the chair is secure and doesn't slide.

Getting Started in Track and Field Athletics

How did I do?
The complicated rules of placing in high jump

The athlete that jumps the greatest height is the winner. However, in many competitions, all of the athletes who are left in a competition may fail the next height. If that happens, the Count Back rule is invoked. The jumper with the fewest number of failures at previous heights is determined the winner. If several athletes are tied using that rule, the athlete who has taken the fewest number of jumps is the winner. If the athletes are tied using that rule, the bar is lowered by 1cm and the athletes have another 3 jumps. If those athletes clear that height the bar goes back up and another 3 attempts is granted.

Look at the box below. The letter X means the jumper has failed to clear the height. An "O" equals a clearance. Colin has finished first as he is the only athlete to clear the bar at 1m 15cms. Jimmy and Michael have failed to clear the bar at 1m 15 and are out of the competition. Who finishes 2nd and 3rd? Michael has 5 height failures in the competition, Jimmy has 6 failures. So Michael takes 2nd place.

Name	1metre	1metre 5cms	1metre 10cms	1metre 15cms
Jimmy	O	XXO	XO	XXX
Michael	O	XO	XO	XXX
Colin	XXO	XXO	O	XXO

Getting Started in Track and Field Athletics

Triple Jump

This event is not recommended for the children for which this book has been written. Triple jump can be an amazing event to watch when performed by the world's best athletes. Like the long jump, the triple jump requires the athlete to take a fast run-up. The athlete takes –off from a board which is either 9 or 11m away from the sand-pit. The athlete lands on the runway with the same foot that they took off with—a **hop**. This is followed by a **step**, i.e. you jump then land on the other foot,. The final (3rd phase) is the **jump** and land in the sand-pit. The **hop - step - and jump** as the triple jump was known covers over 18m for the men, 15m for the women.

While this is a recognized and challenging event in track and field, it is only for athletes that have the strength, flexibility, and physical maturity to cope with the extreme forces that the joints and muscles are exposed to. This essentially precludes young children. The potential damage to young knees and ankles is significant and not advised until the athlete is well into puberty.

The Pole Vault

The pole vault is another jumping event that is not recommended for young children. This event requires the athlete to run fast while carrying a long fibre glass pole. The pole is the shoved into "box" that is set into the track. The pole then bends as if you were compressing a spring. As the pole then springs back from its bent position it releases energy that propels the athlete upward. With the pole bent, the athlete throws their legs upward— so that they are upside down—and "rides" the straightening pole upward. As the pole finally straightens the athlete pushes off the pole so that their legs are up and over the bar. This is a very complex series of movements that require excellent speed, strength, coordination, and gymnastic skill.

Getting Started in Track and Field Athletics
The history of pole vault

The earliest recorded evidence (100 A.D) of something that approximated this event is a story from the Greek island of Crete. Having suffered too many terrible deaths in bull fights, young bull fighters decided to protect themselves—and entertain the crowds—by using a long wooden pole to vault over the charging bull.

Dutch farmers needing to cross from one field to the next would use long wooden poles—usually made from Ash trees - to vault ditches. Vaulting started to become a sport and initially it was for distance rather than height. As the emphasis shifted to height, so experimentation with different types of poles took place. Long canes of bamboo replaced stiff wooden poles which, in turn, were replaced by aluminum poles. It is difficult (if not impossible) to compare the achievements of the record holders through this sports evolution as the increasing flexibility of the poles have afforded the athletes a significant advantage over earlier models. One of the greatest innovations was the introduction of the foam landing mats. As the record heights crept ever higher, the athletes were falling (landing) into sand and risking injury (if not, death). The picture below illustrates this risk. The foam landing mats and highly flexible fibre glass poles have literally "vaulted" the records for this event skyward!

The Throwing Events

Getting Started in Track and Field Athletics

Field events

There are four throwing events in track and field athletics:

- Javelin
- Discus
- Hammer
- Shot putt

Each of these events is technically challenging and require the athlete to coordinate speed and raw strength in a series of complex movement patterns. As young children are still developing their strength, their ability to reach a good standard of performance is inhibited.

Javelin

The forces required to throw the javelin a long distance is likely to place stress on the joints (specifically the shoulder and hip) of a young developing body. Also, teaching javelin to a class of young children presents some very serious safety issues. Immature minds do not necessarily behave in responsible ways with sharp javelins! ***As the risks for injury are high, this book does not recommend javelin (using metal javelins) for young children***. The sports equipment market has a number of foam and plastic javelin products that can be safely used if the teacher wishes to introduce this event. It has been my experience, however, that the children will often try to throw the javelin as if it is a baseball (it is afterall, likely to be baseball or cricket season when you teach this sport). The foam and plastic javelins do not allow the "whip-lash" principles of throwing to be effective, i.e. the athlete can throw very hard and the javelin might not go far at all. The foam javelins can stall in the air and not follow the arc that a metal javelin would follow if correctly released.

As inspiration was considered to be one of the ingredients (as mentioned earlier in this book) of sports success, this book will cover the history and some of the intriguing anecdotes of javelin throwing. The author suggests that the athlete expressing interest in javelin throwing join a track club in their teenage years.

Getting Started in Track and Field Athletics

The history of javelin throwing

As with many track and field events, some of the earliest references of javelin throwing can be found in the studies of ancient classics. Homer – in his epic The Iliad – stated that both Hercules and Achilles were adept javelin throwers. The Greek warriors started battles by throwing javelins before starting hand to hand combat. To test these skills in sports competitions, the ancient Olympic Games had javelin throwing at moving targets as one of the key sports.

Ancient javelin throwing has not altered significantly to the modern day event. The key difference is that the Greek warriors would wrap a small leather thong – termed an *Ankyle* - around the shaft of the javelin (which was made of wood) and use it to create flight stability as the javelin was released.

The technique for javelin requires the precise coordination of a fast run-up, firm plant of the foot (as if braking the speed abruptly) then transferring these forces through the hips and elbow. The action is akin to cracking a whip. A Spanish athlete once experimented with a rotation technique (spinning around and around before releasing the javelin). The distances he could throw were extraordinary – in excess of 100m – but were terrifying for spectators as the javelin did not always go where it was supposed to! The IAAF quickly banned this technique.

When the German athlete Uwe Hohn hurled the javelin 104m (1984) the IAAF realised that the javelins could now be thrown out of the field – and possibly into the crowd! The sports scientists decided to shift the centre of gravity of the javelin so that it falls to ground much sooner when released.

Getting Started in Track and Field Athletics

The Discus

This throwing event has an extensive history as recorded in ancient literature and sculptures. *"Phlegyas ... always loved this sport, and used to practise throwing the discus across the (river) Alpheios where the banks are furthest apart, always clearing the river and never getting the discus wet"*
Statius first century AD

Diskos is a Greek word meaning "thing for throwing" and was an important event in the ancient Olympic Games. The discoi (plural of discus) were either stone, lead, or marble and were known to have varied in weight. In to-day's modern event, the men's discus weighs 2kg while women throw a 1kg discus.

This event requires the athlete to spin 1.5 turns creating massive acceleration and speed that is transferred through to the arm. The discus is released at a 38degree angle and this should allow any facing wind to provide sustained lift as the discus moves through the air. ***This event is very complex and is not recommended for young children – primarily because of safety and injury concerns.*** However, the principles of discus could be introduced with using plastic quoits (rings). Athletes with an interest in this event are encouraged to pursue this once they reach their teenage years.

Getting Started in Track and Field Athletics

Rules of discus throwing

- Enter the circle from the front
- Leave the circle from the back after the discus has been released
- The discus must land within a 45degree sector
- The athlete has 2 minutes to take the throw
- The athlete must stay within the throwing circle – if they step outside, it is considered to be a no-throw.
- Each athlete is allowed 3 throws. At a major track and field championship, the top 6 athletes after 3 throws, would be granted an additional 3 throws.
- The athlete with the furthest single throw is declared the winner.

Getting Started in Track and Field Athletics
The Hammer

This throwing event draws its historical origins from 16th century England. Blacksmiths would throw a sledgehammer in competitions with one another. By the mid 19th century, a 16lb ball (a cannonball—also known as a "shot") was attached to a wooden shaft and this was used as the hammer. A few years later, the wooden shaft was replaced by piano wire.

The hammer is a very difficult event as it requires the athlete to generate create speed and control the 16lb shot as they spin around the throwing circle. Inexperienced athletes may find themselves pulled all over the circle as they do not have the strength or technique to control the hammers momentum. It is an impressive achievement to throw the hammer with skill, but it is also a highly dangerous event. A protective throwing cage to stop errant throws from injuring spectators is essential. **This event is not recommended for children!**

Getting Started in Track and Field Athletics
The Shot Put

Shot put is an event that young children can be introduced to as the implements can be adapted to the age of the athlete, and the event can be safely controlled by the coach / teacher. For students in Grades 3—5 there are 1 and 2kg shots on the market that can be used in your program. With all shot put practices and competitions there are a number of safety issues that must be addressed:

• **Demonstrate how the shot should be carried and held**. Cup your hands around the shot and insist that both hands stay like that until the shot is to be thrown. As the shots can be heavy, they may slip out of a single hand and fall on the athlete's foot. A 16lb adult shot would probably break bones if it landed on the foot. I sometimes impress this point by dropping the shot and letting the athletes hear the "thud" as it hits the ground—note the deep impression in the ground this can make.

• **Insist that all shot puts are returned to the throwing circle by the athlete that has thrown it**. Do not allow the next athlete into the throwing circle until the area is completely clear.

• **The shots can be destructive to a sports field with impact craters forming very quickly**. If you do not have a designated throwing area and to preserve your field, have the children throw into the long jump pit. You can mark out a throwing circle with cones.

Getting Started in Track and Field Athletics

The history of shot put

Many track and field events have their historical origins in the ancient Olympic Games but shot put is an exception. The Greeks took great interest in the artistry of the athletic event; for them, looking good was just as important as being a good athlete. The discus and javelin events were considered by the Greeks to be "beautiful events." Shot put, however, seemed to be more of a test of brute strength rather than skill (something in today's athletics that couldn't be more false). Consequently, shot put was not considered part of the ancient Olympic Games.

Historically, the next references for the shot put event come from Europe in the medieval period. Young man were challenged to throw very heavy stones "manhood stones" to prove that you were no longer a child. Throwing stones in competitions, or long poles of wood—Tossing the Caber— were an important part of athletic competitions in 18th and 19th century Scotland. It is from Scotland that Shot Put acquired its name. An old Scottish verb "Put" was applied in throwing events to mean thrust." The shot was the British Navy term for a heavy cannonball—generally weighing 16lbs.

The techniques for throwing the shot have not changed significantly over the years. A standing throw—leaning back and then heaving the ball into the air was replaced by the more technical Glide technique (also known as the O'Brien technique). The rotational technique—where the athlete spins around the circle before releasing the shot was termed the Baryshnikov technique. In today's modern athletics, athletes primarily use the glide, with a few using the rotational.

Track Trivia

There was, however, a competition known as the Lithobolos where athletes attempted to throw huge stones above their heads with one hand. At the museum in Olympia (Greece) there is a stone weighing 316 lbs (143 kg) that has a plaque next to it that has the inscription :

"Bubon .. Threw me over his head!"

Getting Started in Track and Field Athletics

Rules of shot put

- The shot must land within the sector marked out on the field (a 45 degree sector).

- The shot must be pushed not thrown like a baseball.

- The length of the throw is from the edge of the throwing circle to where the shot lands (not stops rolling!)

- Each athlete is allowed 3 throws (although the top 6 at an international championship will be granted an additional 3 throws).

- The winner of the competition is the athlete with the furthest throw. You do not add the distances of the 3 throws together!

- The athlete must enter and leave the throwing circle from the back, if you leave from the front the throw will not count.

- Athletes who touch the top of the stop-board will make their throw invalid.

- Each athlete has two minutes to make the throw. Longer than two minutes and the throw is not allowed.

- The athlete may skip a throw—but they will not be allowed to take it at a later time in the competition.

Getting Started in Track and Field Athletics

Common mistakes made in shot put

Young children will try to throw the shot like a baseball and, naturally, they will not have the strength to execute this action successfully.

Walking out of the front of the throwing circle (and thus making the throw invalid) is a very common mistake and the children will need to get used to this rule.

The glide technique can be mastered but sometimes presents difficulties when the athlete tries to turn the wrong way. From the starting position the athlete hops back then turns and pushes the shot. Remind the children that if they start with their right leg forward they must turn left once they have powerfully hopped backwards.

Shot Put activities
Throw for points

Split your athletes / students into several groups. Mark out on the throwing area zones (use tape or rope). A shot that is thrown into the closest zone to the throwing circle earns the least number of points. For every zone, increase the number of points that can be earned. Keep track of each throw and have a team competition for points.

Getting Started in Track and Field Athletics

Overhead throwing competitions

The athlete stands with their back to the edge of the throwing circle. With both hands firmly cupping the shot, they swing the shot upwards and backwards so that the shot flies out onto the landing sector. Make sure that all spectators are at least 20 feet away in all directions from an athlete doing this activity. You can make this a competitive activity by going for distance, or making it a team event by using the zone for points approach described above.

Underswing competitions

Face the shot put throwing sector with both hands firmly cupping the shot. The athlete bends their knees and swings the shot upward and outward. The shot is released at the height of the arc. The shot will fly outward and land in the throwing sector. As with activities described above, this can used for individual and team competitions.

Questions parents ask...

My child is very strong and can handle a heavier shot...

Of course there is considerable variance in the natural strength of pre-pubertal children and it may well be the case that a particular child could use a heavier shot. One of the key premises of this book is that skill acquisition is far more important with this age –group than performance outcome. This strong child will learn the principles of technique—and throwing events are very technical— much easier with a lighter shot than a much heavier one. Performing with a heavier shot may result in a deterioration in the skill learning as the athlete struggles to cope with the extra weight.

Learn the skills first, there will be plenty of time to show the world how strong you are later!

Getting Started in Track and Field Athletics

Aren't these children a bit young for learning an event such as shot put?

Essentially, what I am trying to do with this book is to introduce young kids to possibilities that track and field present. The history and rules of the sport have been covered in this book so that the children can understand and appreciate this event should they see it on television or being performed live.

A well designed track and field program will give a sample of these events to young and interested athletes. To specifically answer this important question, I would remind the parent / coach that the emphasis is on having fun with the skill and not a strict training regime for the next Olympic shot put champion!

Teachers Corner

Designing a safe environment requires some experience and the firm reinforcing of basic safety practices. As mentioned at the beginning of the shot putt section, have your athletes carry the shots out with two hands. Ideally, the safest means of teaching this event is to have the children line up and one at a time throw just one shot. Of course, with a large class this is not a practical means of teaching. You might like to give each a large softball and teach the principles of the glide technique—space the children a minimum 10m apart and insist that they put the ball at the same time. When you are throwing the shots, have all of your athletes 15 metres away and outside the throwing sector. No athlete should be standing inside the throwing sector. Note that even the most experienced of track and field judges will stand outside this sector when the athlete is throwing—you wouldn't want to be hit in the head with a 16lb cannonball!

World records

The children love to see how their performances compare with the world records. Even though they will not be using the adult weight shots, pull out a tape measure and show them these records:

Men's World record: Randy Barnes USA 23m.12cms
Women's World Record: Natayla Lisovskaya Russia - 22m.63cms

The Hurdle events

Getting Started in Track and Field Athletics

The Hurdle events

There are three types of hurdles races in track athletics:

- The steeplechase
- The High hurdles—110m for men, 100m for women
- The 400m hurdles

The Steeplechase

The steeplechase is a combination of a distance and hurdle race. Athletes run either 2000 or 3000m and hurdle barriers set at 90cms in height. This is a new event that women participate in at the championship level. competitions are held with the barrier height set at 76cms. Steeplechase requires the athlete to hurdle 4 barriers, and 1 water jump for each lap. The water jump is a pit dug into the track (usually on the side of the track) and is slanted. At the end of the pit – closest to the barrier – it is at its deepest (0.70m). The furthest point away from the barrier is the shallowest part of the pit. The incentive, then, is for the athlete to jump as far as possible and avoid getting completely wet. A few athletes have been known to clear the water jump without even putting their foot in the water. This can be a challenging event as the rhythm of a distance race is being continually broken by the athlete having to hurdle these barriers. Training for this event is primarily from a distance running perspective, but good hurdling technique helps to minimize the athlete's fatigue.

Getting Started in Track and Field Athletics

The History of Steeplechasing

This event takes its origins from the English tradition of cross country running. Students in English public schools would be sent out on a "paper chase." This was where an athlete would be sent out to run across fields, through forests, wherever they wanted run. This runner would leave a trail of torn paper pieces for the other athletes to follow. Sometimes the lead runner would try to lead the followers astray by laying down a false trail. Often the chasers (this race was also known as Hare and Hounds) would have to jump over fences, ditches, gates, etc in their attempts to catch the leader. It is from this that the steeplechase evolved.

> ## Questions children ask...
> ### *Why can't I do the steeplechase?*
> The hurdle height for steeplechase is too high, and the distance to be run too long for the athletes for which this book is written. Teenagers have the opportunity to run 1500m steeplechase (3 and 3/4 laps of the track).

Getting Started in Track and Field Athletics

Hurdles

The successful hurdler will need to bring excellent:

• **Speed**. Good technique is essential but no amount of technical skill can replace the necessity for sprinting speed. This is a sprinting race and the athlete's speed between the hurdles (combined with speed over the hurdle) will determine how well the athlete does.

• **Flexibility** (especially in the hips) is needed to help the athlete rotate their leg and achieve the hurdle position (as shown in the graphic below).

• **Coordination** (so as to efficiently clear all the hurdles with good technique), good balance (so that after landing from the previous hurdle clearance, the athlete can go straight into their running and approach the next hurdle)

• **Timing** – this will allow the runner to takeoff and clear the hurdle without crashing into it.

• **Rhythm** – the hurdles is a rhythm event. Knocking down a hurdle breaks this rhythm and inhibits performance.

Track -talk

In the sprint hurdles race, the men run 110m while the women race over 100m for women. The heights of the hurdles are 42" for men, 30" for women.

Getting Started in Track and Field Athletics

The technique of hurdling

The leg that goes over the hurdle first is known as the lead leg, the one that follows is known as the trail leg. Perhaps one of the most common mistakes made by young athletes attempting this event for the first time is that they tend to jump over the hurdle. The goal for hurdling is to clear the barrier as quickly as possible so that the sprinting can resume; jumping the hurdle slows the sprinting time. The athlete can only sprint when they are in contact with the track, time spent in the air is time wasted. The hurdler aims to clear the barrier by the narrowest of margins without knocking it over. If hit, the hurdle can break the rhythm of the runner and may slow them down.

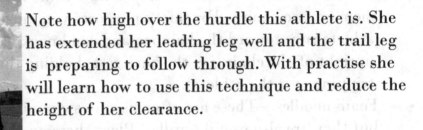

Note how high over the hurdle this athlete is. She has extended her leading leg well and the trail leg is preparing to follow through. With practise she will learn how to use this technique and reduce the height of her clearance.

Questions children ask...

What if you hit a hurdle, or knock it over, are you disqualified?

Before metal hurdles, light wooden barriers were used in competitions. Athletes could knock these hurdles over quite easily and it had very little effect on their sprinting speed. The track judges then issued a rule that disqualified an athlete for knocking the hurdles over. This rule was changed with the introduction of metal hurdles. An athlete will not be disqualified (as long as they attempt to hurdle the barrier) if they knock them over. Hitting them is not an advantage as they can slow the sprinter down significantly.

Track-talk

The hurdles in 400metre hurdles race 36" high and 35m apart. For women they are 30" high and 35m apart

---

Getting Started in Track and Field Athletics

Adaptations for young children

This is a very popular event for young kids and there are several ways that you can adapt this to fit the age and skill level of your group. There are a number of products on the sports equipment market that will help you. Some of this equipment is very expensive and there are a number of simple (but cheap) innovations that can serve the same purpose:

- Foam hurdles — These can be very effective for young children. You can buy them in a number of different heights and they allow the children to gain some confidence with this event. The only problem here is that they tend to be very expensive.
- Bamboo canes over chairs— If you have some thin bamboo canes place them on two chairs. For safety purposes you must ensure that the athlete runs toward the bamboo and can knock it off without the upright of the chair (i.e. the back rest) holding the cane in place (and tripping over the athlete).
- Foam noodles - These are often used in swimming pools for fun games but they are also useful hurdles. Place them on chairs and again make sure the athlete runs toward them.
- Junior hurdles (see picture) - In the picture on the previous page, you will see a simple hurdle set that can be adjusted in height according to the skills and age of your athletes. These are expensive to buy however.

Getting Started in Track and Field Athletics

400m hurdles

This event is not recommended for the students for which this book is written, the combination of hurdling and sprinting 400m will be too challenging for this age group. Athletes who do take part in this event have to apply a range of complex skills that include different stride patterns between the hurdles, hurdling technique, sprinting speed, and speed endurance.

The World Records

100m Hurdles for women — 12.21 seconds by Yordanka Donkova Bulgaria

110m Hurdles for men—12.91 seconds by Colin Jackson— Great Britain

400m Hurdles for women— 52.61 seconds by Kim Batten USA

400m Hurdles for men—46.78 seconds by Kevin Young—

The Amazing Robert Tisdall

For many athletes they only have one chance at an Olympic Games to stake their claim for a gold medal. As the 1932 Los Angeles Olympics approached Robert Tisdall—an Irishman attending Cambridge University—decided to suspend his studies and devote all of his time to running. He spent every penny that he had training and so had to live in a railway carriage. At the games, Tisdall won his race and broke the world record for the 400m hurdles. However, he knocked over the final hurdle and according to the rule of the day was not allowed to hold the record. The man in 2nd place also broke the record. It is the only time in sport that the man in 1st place was not the record holder but the man in 2nd place was! Robert Tisdall was this author's great Uncle.

Getting Started in Track and Field Athletics

Multi Events

Track and field athletics provides competition for those athletes that wish to combine the disciplines of a number of different events. The men can compete in what is known as the Decathlon. This is a 10 event competition that must be held over two days. It includes the following: 100m, long jump, shot put, pole vault, high hurdles, 400m, discus, javelin, high jump, and 1500m. The athletes are given a number of points (based on a complex scoring system) for each performance. The athlete with the most points at the end of the competition wins.

The multi event competition for women is known as the Heptathlon. This is an 8 event that includes: 100m, 200m, long jump, high jump, 100m hurdles, javelin, shot put, and 800m. As with the men, points are awarded and the winner is the athlete with the highest total.

The origins of multi-event competitions

As the ancient Olympic Games were a means to test the skills of Greek warriors, it seems natural that they would want to measure the all-round capabilities of their athletes over several events. The ancient games held the Pentathlon competition. This included running, wrestling, jumping, the discus and the javelin.

The running races were particularly challenging. In one race the warriors were expected to run 4 stades (laps around the stadium) - a distance of about 800m—carrying their body armour. With helmet and shield, this could amount to 50—60 lbs.

Wrestling events — a test of combat skill and strength— also carried a rule that allowed you to break the fingers of your opponent. No such rule exists in today's Olympics!

Warriors competing in the long jump used Halteres—stone weights—to help them gain extra distance.

Getting Started in Track and Field Athletics

Multi- events and young children

Young children maybe interested in a multi-event concept and consistent with the theme of developing a broad range of athletic skills before specializing, you might want to consider this format: Run - Jump - Throw. Have each child run a 100m, perform a long jump, and throw a shot put (choose the weight appropriate to the age). Take the 100m time and subtract it from 100m. For the long jump and shot, the performance counts as 1 point for each centimeter of distance. For example:

Mary runs 100m in 18. 0 seconds = 182 points
She long jumps 3m 22cms   = 322 points
She throws the shot 5m 19cms   = 519 points
                    Total = 1023 points

The next time Mary takes part she has a score that she can try to improve. Other schools adopting similar scoring systems would allow for a multi-event competition to be held across great distances.

The Internet Track and Field Challenge

As technology increasingly enters the educational establishment and the family home, it has allowed for some innovative ways to disseminate knowledge and generate interest in a particular activity. Using a straight forward data-base, athletes at my school will repeatedly run a 100m, 800m and do the long jump. Times / distances are recorded and then entered into the data base. Schools from other parts of the country do the same. The computer programme then ranks the athletes. Students can visit the website and see how they compare with other athletes in a "virtual track meet." This event takes place for one month. Students can attempt to improve their ranking. The programme adjusts the rankings accordingly. At the end of the month, all times and positions are final and the track and field meet is over. Not only does this format integrate technology into the physical education curriculum, but it also promotes interest in track and field amongst athletes are usually disinclined to participate. The website features articles, tips, and features designed to develop the athletes / coaches knowledge of the sport.

Visit: www.smus.ca/trackmeet

Getting Started in Track and Field Athletics

Race Walking

Race walking is a demanding event that requires the athlete to compete for up to 5 hours (in the 50km event). Thus, it is the longest of the track and field events surpassing the marathon which is 42 km. Race walking is particularly challenging, for not only does it require excellent endurance and co-ordination, but the athlete must suppress the desire to break into a run. The rules are strictly enforced in this event; an athlete's foot must always be in contact with the ground. If both feet are judged to be "in the air" the athlete is deemed to be running (or lifting as it is called). The athlete will receive one warning for lifting and will be disqualified on the second infraction.

What are the origins of race walking?

In the 12th century the employees (indentured slaves) of very wealthy people (Kings, Lords, Dukes, Earls, etc) in England were expected to follow their master's horsedrawn coach on foot. Thus they became known as "footmen." They alternated between running and walking matching the varying speed of the carriages as it moved across the country. It was from this that a tradition of competition amongst footmen started to emerge. In the 1800's vast sums of money were wagered on walking competitions (later called Pedestrianism) that could last up to six days. (See the story of Captain Barclay on page90). At the modern Olympic Games, the competitive distances have varied. Currently, they are set at 20km for men and women and an additional race of 50km for men only.

Race Walking and young children

This is an excellent activity for students whom may find running to be difficult. The training principles and racing distances can be directly copied from the middle distance running section of this book. Thus, it is recommended that students from grades 3—6 race walk in distances ranging from 800m to 1.5 km

Getting Started in Track and Field Athletics

Acknowledgements

This project would not have been possible without the financial assistance of my employer **St. Michaels University School,** Victoria, British Columbia, Canada. Thank you for your support in fulfilling a dream.

My sincere thanks is extended to the following people:

Mr. Dave Gilmore for his time and exceptional skill with the camera.

The young athletes at **SMUS** for helping to shape the ideas that form the core of this book.

Mr. Barry Tompkins for all his technical support throughout this project.

A special thanks to my family, **Michelle, Michael and Colin**— for forgiving me for all the hours at the computer! And finally, to my parents Maureen and Brian for their unfailing support throughout my running career.

Author Biography

Gary Barber is a school teacher at St. Michaels University School, British Columbia, Canada. He was an international track athlete in the 1500m. He is the author of the book "**Sports Psychology for Runners.**"

His first running race was at the age of 3 against a young girl with a massive ginger afro (as was the style in those days). If you are reading this ... I still think you cheated and I want a re-match!

This book is dedicated to the memory of Simon Rodhouse

A great athlete, a fabulous mentor…. My old PE teacher...

Printed in the United States
by Baker & Taylor Publisher Services